DARWIN'S NOTEBOOK

DARWIN'S NOTEBOOK

The Life, Times, and Discoveries of

Charles Robert Darwin

Written and Compiled by
JONATHAN CLEMENTS

Running Press
Philadelphia • London

© 2009 by Quid Publishing

First published in the United States in 2009
by Running Press Book Publishers

9   8   7   6   5   4   3   2   1

Digit on the right indicates the number of this printing

Library of Congress Control Number:
2008944126

ISBN: 978-0-7624-3776-4

Conceived, designed, and produced by
Quid Publishing
Level 4, Sheridan House,
114 Western Road,
Hove,
BN3 1DD
England
www.quidpublishing.com

Design by: Lindsey Johns

Running Press Book Publishers
2300 Chestnut St.
Philadelphia, PA 19103-4371

Visit us on the web!
www.runningpress.com

Contents

Introduction

THE YOUNG CHARLES DARWIN WAS DERIDED AS A DISGRACE, REGARDED AS AN IDLE RICH BOY WITH LITTLE APTITUDE FOR ANYTHING EXCEPT COUNTRY LIFE. IT SEEMS ODD, AND SEEMED STRANGE EVEN TO DARWIN, THAT HE ONCE CONSIDERED A LIFE AS A CLERGYMAN, AND MIGHT WELL HAVE ENDED UP AS A BEETLE-COLLECTING COUNTRY PARSON, WERE IT NOT FOR A SUDDEN AND UNEXPECTED OPPORTUNITY. SAILING AROUND THE WORLD ABOARD HMS *BEAGLE* LEFT DARWIN WITH A LIFETIME OF IDEAS AND THEORIES, AND CREATED ONE OF THE GIANTS OF 19TH-CENTURY SCIENCE.

Despite Darwin's fame, he is often remembered for the wrong reasons. Charles Darwin did not invent the theory of evolution. The idea of transmutation, or transformation from one species to another had been around long before him, and had even been suggested by his grandfather. Darwin's achievement was not in the idea of evolution itself, but in his explanation of it. He was not the inventor of the theory of evolution; he was the inventor of the theory of natural selection.

Even during his lifetime Darwin was misunderstood and misrepresented. In 1864, he was awarded the prestigious Copley Medal, but pointedly it was in recognition of works other than his controversial *On the Origin of Species* (1859). Upon his death, he was buried in Westminster Abbey, London, despite his loss of faith in the Anglican Church, and largely in an attempt by the British establishment to expiate its own guilt, having failed to honor Darwin while he was alive.

It was natural selection, as set out in *On the Origin of Species*, which caused such a stir in scientific circles, and continues to provoke heated discussion a century and a half later. For the first time, a thinker had suggested not *that* evolution existed, but *why* it existed, and how it might work. Most crucially, it was an explanation that required no supernatural agency, no divine Creator, nor Biblical authority. Darwin's simple idea threatened the very foundations of the religious establishment, and the widely held belief that nature existed for the benefit of humankind.

Just as Copernicus, in the mid-16th century, had challenged the notion that the Earth was at the center of the universe, Darwin's theory of natural selection painted humankind as part of nature, not its ruler. But like Copernicus, Darwin knew how controversial the implications of his theory would be, which was why he initially intended not to allow the publication of his ideas until after he was safely in his grave.

A Life's Work

On the Origin of Species was Darwin's life's work; however, it was far from being his only contribution to science. Two of his best-known later books, *The Descent of Man* (1871) and *The Expression of Emotions* (1872), began life as part of *Origin*, but were hived off for lack of space. Darwin intended to publish them as articles, but they became books in their own right.

Shut away in his study, the victim of a debilitating and embarrassing ailment that kept him largely out of the public eye, Darwin lived for writing and little else. He was a prolific author, and although he is best remembered for his work on evolution and natural selection, he is feted in

Darwin is usually depicted with his distinctive, bushy beard, although this Victorian adornment only arrived in the 1860s. Before that point, he was clean-shaven.

"I have called this principle, by which each slight variation, if useful, is preserved, by the term of Natural Selection, in order to mark its relation to man's power of selection."

— On the Origin of Species by Means of Natural Selection, 1859

many other disciplines including geology and botany. He discovered dozens of species of beetles and birds; he became the world authority on barnacles; he offered theories that would later form the foundations of disciplines such as cosmology and sociobiology, and is even considered a spiritual ancestor of psychology.

In the decades since his death, Darwin's theories have been debated, co-opted, and refined. They have been used for both good and ill—in the 20th century, they were corrupted in order to justify many of humanity's worst atrocities in the cause of eugenics. As Darwin once noted, when faced with what humans could do to each other, sometimes he might have preferred to be a "heroic little monkey."

The influence of Darwin's ideas is inescapable: the work of this great man has fundamentally changed our concept of who we are and where we come from.

CHAPTER ONE

EARLY LIFE
AND
SCHOOLING

The Descent of Darwin

BEFORE WE MEET CHARLES DARWIN HIMSELF, IT IS INSTRUCTIONAL TO LOOK AT HIS ANCESTORS. ONE OF DARWIN'S GRANDFATHERS WAS A PHYSICIAN AND INVENTOR WHO WROTE EPIC POEMS ABOUT THE POLLINATION OF PLANTS. THE OTHER WAS A WEALTHY FACTORY OWNER. BOTH WERE ANTI-SLAVERY CAMPAIGNERS, WHOSE ATTITUDES MADE A STRONG ENOUGH IMPRESSION ON THEIR CHILDREN THAT THEY WOULD PASS IT ON TO YET ANOTHER GENERATION—DARWIN'S OWN.

In later life, Darwin wrote that he wished his grandfather had left some essay or article to posterity that would give his descendants some idea of the formation of his character. The man to which he was referring was his paternal grandfather, Erasmus Darwin, a puckish figure of the 18th century who championed steam engines and the "rights of man," and even privately questioned the truth of the Bible.

The Scientific Poet

Erasmus Darwin (1731–1802) was a physician from Newark in Nottinghamshire, England, who had found local fame in Lichfield when he cured a young man thought to be on the verge of death. Running a successful practice as a doctor, Erasmus turned down the offer to become Royal Physician to King George III, and instead tinkered with inventions and wrote several minor works of scientific philosophy.

When he discovered that British botanists were censoring translations of the Swedish botanist Linnaeus, taking out any suggestion that plants might have male and female elements, Erasmus regarded the decision as a grave mistake. In protest, he wrote a long poem in heroic couplets, *The Loves of the Plants*, deliberately describing the pollination of flowers in romantic terms—racy by the standards of his day.

Darwin's family believed that Erasmus was one of the bystanders depicted in the 1768 Joseph Wright painting *An Experiment on a Bird in an Air Pump*.

Typically for the attitudes of his day, Charles Darwin seems to have given little thought to the inheritance he may have received from his grandmothers. Mary Howard, wife of Erasmus, drank herself into an early grave aged 31. Emma Wedgwood, wife of Josiah, shared his surname because she was a distant cousin.

Entity of Entities

Erasmus Darwin believed in the existence of God, or *Ens Entium* (Entity of Entities), but saw no reason to attribute a role to the Creator of the Universe in the day-to-day running of Creation.

"That there exists a superior Ens Entium, which formed these wonderful creatures, is a mathematical demonstration," he wrote in 1754. "That HE influences things by a particular providence is not so evident. The probability, according to my notion, is against it, since general laws seem sufficient for that end. Shall we say no particular providence is necessary to roll this Planet round the Sun…?"

Living Filament

Erasmus went a step farther in his *Zoönomia* (1794), when he suggested that God was a First Cause, setting the Universe in motion, but that after that, Creation had been left to run and improve itself. Animals, thought Erasmus, had a God-given ability to change over many generations into other animals.

"[I]n the great length of time, since the earth began to exist, perhaps millions of ages before the commencement of the history of mankind, would it be too bold to imagine that all warm-blooded animals have … the power of acquiring new parts, attended with new propensities, directed by irritations, sensations, volitions, and associations, and thus possessing the faculty of continuing to improve … and of delivering down those improvements by generation to its posterity, world without end!"

The Potter's Wheel

Both Darwin's grandfathers agreed on the matter of slavery, which they found to be a terrible indictment of "civilized" society, and were determined to see abolished. Erasmus wrote angry verses about it, while his other grandfather Josiah Wedgwood (1730–95) designed an anti-slavery slogan in porcelain.

Having lost a leg to smallpox as a youth, Wedgwood had been unable to operate a potter's wheel, and so turned to pottery design, industrializing porcelain with the establishment of the famous Wedgwood factory. With the help of his wife's family fortune, he became an even wealthier man, and was even admitted to the Royal Society, after inventing a device for measuring the temperature within furnaces.

EXTRACT FROM *THE LOVES OF THE PLANTS* BY ERASMUS DARWIN

Botanic muse! who in this
  latter age
Led by your airy hand the
  Swedish sage,
Bade his keen eye your secret
  haunts explore
On dewy dell, high wood, and
  winding shore;
Say on each leaf how tiny
  Graces dwell;
How laugh the Pleasures in a
  blossom's bell;
How insect loves arise on
  cobweb wings,
Aim their light shafts, and point
  their little stings.

Note: The "Swedish sage" to whom Erasmus Darwin refers is Carolus Linnaeus, the botanist who introduced the system of binomial nomenclature for defining and naming organisms.

So Simple a Beginning

CHARLES DARWIN WAS THE SECOND-YOUNGEST CHILD OF THE PHYSICIAN ROBERT DARWIN AND SUSANNAH WEDGWOOD, AN HEIRESS TO THE WEALTH OF THE WEDGWOOD POTTERY EMPIRE. HE GREW UP IN THE TOWN OF SHREWSBURY IN WESTERN ENGLAND, DOTED ON BY HIS ELDER SISTERS, AND WAITED UPON BY SERVANTS.

Erasmus Darwin and Josiah Wedgwood were good friends, even if they argued about religion. Wedgwood was a Unitarian, believing that Jesus Christ had been a great prophet and a great man, but was not literally the embodiment of God. The idea had once been heresy, but was now gaining ground among many Christians.

Erasmus scoffed at the idea, not because he was a member of the Church of England, but because he did not believe in much of the Bible at all. The Entity of Entities was enough for him, and he regarded Wedgwood's Unitarianism as "a feather bed to catch a falling Christian"—implying that he expected Wedgwood was already on a course toward agnosticism or even atheism.

The two men eventually arranged a marriage between two of their children. Robert Darwin, youngest son of Erasmus, would marry Susannah, eldest daughter of Wedgwood, although the father of the prospective bride insisted that his daughter would not walk up the aisle until Robert had demonstrated that he was worthy of her. This criterion—a matter of financial stability—was not fulfilled until after Josiah's death.

Darwin's Parents

Like his father, Robert Darwin was a doctor. He studied medicine in Edinburgh and at the old Dutch university of Leiden; and developed views that were modern enough to regard the practice of bleeding patients as barbaric. He was a successful man, so much so that he was also able to lend money to local people by the hundreds, even thousands of pounds. The income

Darwin's father, Robert, the wealthy (and weighty) country doctor.

The family trees of the Darwins and Wedgwoods, showing the close relation of Charles to his future wife Emma.

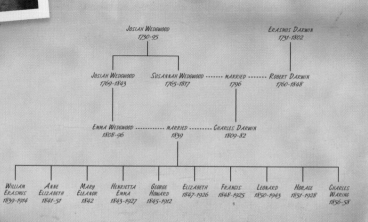

"I think memory of events commences abruptly, that is I remember these earliest things quite as clearly as others very much later in life."

from his thriving surgery, along with inheritances from Erasmus and two deceased aunts, meant that Robert was finally deemed fit to marry the heiress Susannah in 1796.

The couple had six children—four girls and two boys. The most famous, Charles Robert Darwin, was their fifth child, born on February 12, 1809, coincidentally the same day as Abraham Lincoln. He grew up with three significantly elder sisters, Marianne, Caroline, and Susan, an elder brother also named Erasmus (Ras or Eras), and a younger sister Emily.

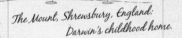

The Mount

Darwin's childhood home was The Mount, a modern residence built in red brick to his father's specifications, at what was then the edge of the growing town of Shrewsbury. The house was designed both as a residence and a place of work—Robert's patients would turn left as they entered the main hall to reach a purpose-built doctor's surgery. Outbuildings included servants' quarters, stables, and the tool house where the Darwin brothers would set up their first laboratory. Robert Darwin himself kept a "garden diary," observing the plants in his grounds, and would eventually add a greenhouse in 1832.

The Mount, Shrewsbury, England: Darwin's childhood home.

First Memories

Charles Darwin believed that the first event he could reasonably recall was sitting on the knee of his sister Caroline, while she cut an orange for him. Startled by the sudden appearance of a cow near the window, the infant Darwin flinched, causing Caroline to cut him with the knife—leaving a scar that he would carry for the rest of his life. After that, he remembered a trip to the seaside aged four, although notably he could only remember the maidservants who cared for him, and not the parents who must have taken him. Other early memories, however, only survived as mere fragments or emotions, such as his pride and vanity when he thought adults were watching him climb an ash tree in the garden.

Darwin's other recollections of his early childhood largely revolved around safety, such as a dire warning not to walk "on the wrong side of the horse." The saying reflects the all-but-forgotten custom of using a horse to pull a barge along a canal, and the danger of finding oneself caught between the tow-rope and the edge of the water.

The English castle town of Shrewsbury sits near the historic border with Wales.

Childhood's End

DARWIN'S RECOLLECTIONS OF HIS OWN CHILDHOOD WERE FILTERED THROUGH THE DISCIPLINE OF A SCIENTIST. HE WAS INTERESTED NOT ONLY IN HIS MEMORIES, BUT IN THE GAPS IN HIS MENTAL RECORD. TRUE TO HIS ADULT BELIEF THAT MUCH HUMAN NATURE WAS PREDETERMINED IN THE WOMB, HE BELIEVED HE HAD BEEN BORN WITH AN INNATE INTEREST IN COLLECTING AND CLASSIFYING.

As an adult, Darwin believed that many human memories were artificial constructions. Rather than an archive of recorded experiences, he believed that many memories were formed "from hearing the thing so often repeated, one obtains so vivid an image that it cannot be separated from memory."

This theory helps explain why Darwin could recall so little about his own mother, Susannah, who died when he was just eight years old. Darwin remembered very little beyond the sight of her black velvet gown, and the memory of walking by her side. He would later attribute this lack of recall to his sisters' deep grief, and their refusal to talk about their mother after her untimely death. Darwin believed that, despite being old enough to remember many earlier incidents, such as the celebrations after the Battle of Waterloo (1815), his recollections of his mother were almost entirely wiped out by the lack of revision provided by other family members.

"I scarcely recollect anything, except for being sent for — memory of going into her room, my Father meeting us crying afterwards."

A Passion for Collecting

Darwin was taught by his sister Caroline at home until shortly after his mother's death. He then attended a day-school, where he soon discovered a boyish zeal for collecting strange objects. "I tried to make out the names of plants," he wrote, "and collected all sorts of things, shells, seals, franks, coins and minerals." He attempted to classify all the pebbles to be found near the entrance to his school, and became a keen and experimental gardener. On one occasion, the young Darwin boasted to

"The passion for collecting, which leads a man to be a systematic naturalist, a virtuoso or a miser, was very strong in me, and clearly innate as none of my sisters or brother ever had this taste."

the other children that he could change the color of crocuses by watering them with dye. When he repeated the story in later life, it was to his great embarrassment, not because it was an outrageous lie, but because he had not tested his hypothesis before bragging about it.

The young Darwin developed a family reputation for long, solitary walks. A trip to Wales found him despondent if stuck with his sisters, but blissfully happy if allowed to wander along the beach looking for stones and shells.

A Fall on the Wall

Shrewsbury was once Scrobbesburh, the "fort on the scrubland," to the ancient Anglo-Saxons, and had always been a castle town. The young Darwin was once so preoccupied in his wanderings along the footpath near the ruined town walls, he walked right off the edge of a precipice, and fell a terrifying but ultimately harmless eight feet (2.4 meters). His memory of the incident, as ever, recalls more scientific enquiry than fear.

"Nevertheless," he observed, "the number of thoughts which passed through my mind during this very short but sudden and wholly unexpected fall, was astonishing, and seemed hardly compatible with what physiologists have, I believe, proved about each thought requiring quite an appreciable amount of time."

Boarding School

In 1818, Darwin was sent away to a boarding school, albeit still in Shrewsbury. The schoolmaster, Samuel Butler (whose son would feud with Darwin many decades later), subjected Darwin to a tortuous regime of Latin and Greek studies that he soon forgot. Although he displayed a greater interest in the English works of Shakespeare and Byron, his heart was already devoted to the rarer and less "gentlemanly" pursuit of science.

"In figure he was bulky and heavy-looking, and did not then manifest any powers of mind. He was reserved in manner, & we thought him proud, insomuch as he did not join in any play with the other boys but went straight home from school."

—— WILLIAM ALLPORT LEIGHTON, CLASSMATE

Charles Robert Darwin aged nine.

The Scientist

ONE OF CHARLES DARWIN'S MOST IMPORTANT EARLY RELATIONSHIPS WAS WITH HIS ELDER BROTHER ERASMUS. OUTNUMBERED BY THEIR SISTERS, THE DARWIN BOYS BECAME INSEPARABLE. DARWIN IDOLIZED "RAS," REGARDING HIM AS A "SOCIABLE AND PLEASANT" MAN. SHORTLY BEFORE ERASMUS LEFT SHREWSBURY FOR CAMBRIDGE UNIVERSITY, THE BOYS BEGAN CONDUCTING AMATEUR EXPERIMENTS IN A GARDEN SHED.

"Nothing could have been worse for the development of my mind," wrote Darwin, "than Dr. Butler's school, as it was strictly classical, nothing else being taught except a little ancient geography and history."

The focus on the school was on learning by rote, a task at which Darwin succeeded for 48-hour stretches, only to entirely forget what he had learned. He pronounced himself an utter failure at languages, and survived with the aid of a secret concoction of ready-made phrases, which the boys would swap around in order to construct ready-made Latin verse compositions.

Snipe Hunting

As a teenager, Darwin developed a sudden interest in shooting, and would often go out hunting. "How well I remember killing my first snipe," he enthused, "and my excitement was so great that I had great difficulty in reloading my gun from the trembling of my hands."

Darwin's Laboratory

When not at the school, Darwin and his older brother Erasmus would tinker with chemistry in a tool shed, heating chemical compounds, growing crystals, and measuring minerals. Their chemistry set was assembled at some expense; the boys joked that getting money out of their father was like "milking a cow," although the Wedgwood relatives helped out by sending some of their patented fireproof porcelain. Darwin even carried on these experiments back at boarding school, standing close to

"I do not believe that anyone could have shown more zeal for the most holy cause than I did for shooting birds."

The common snipe or fantail snipe (*Gallinago gallinago*).

"What I shall buy in London will be principally stop cocks & jars with stop cocks..."

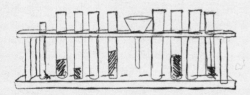

his dormitory gaslight with a handful of chemical compounds, ready to fling them into the flames. For this pursuit, he gained the schoolboy nickname "Gas."

"I was once also publicly rebuked by the head-master, Dr. Butler," remembered Darwin, "for thus wasting my time over such useless subjects; and he called me very unjustly a 'poco curante' [from the Italian for 'caring little'] and as I did not understand what he meant it seemed to me to be a fearful reproach."

Solo Science

Darwin continued his experiments even after Erasmus left for Cambridge, shadowing his brother's early scientific studies, and reporting back on the state of the "laboratory." Meanwhile, Erasmus wrote to Charles with words of encouragement, suggestions of new experiments to try, and reports of some of the more exciting scientific shenanigans at his college. These included the delirious effects of nitrous oxide (laughing gas), which Erasmus recommended his brother try for himself.

Darwin was plainly taking his chemistry very seriously. One letter from Erasmus notes that the boys had commissioned glassblowers to make test tubes to a specific size, only to have the artisans send them useless, flat-bottomed versions.

"What I shall buy in London," wrote Erasmus, "will be principally stop cocks & jars with stop cocks, for that is what we are principally deficient in."

Darwin regarded his experiments as the most important and enduring part of his education. However, his father was less impressed with the scientific games, although he did admit that Dr. Butler's curriculum seemed to be achieving little with his wayward son.

"As I was doing no good at school," wrote Darwin, "my father wisely took me away at a rather earlier age than usual..."

Darwin's father had decided that his son needed to learn a trade, quite probably a medical one. But whereas Robert Darwin was a self-made man, his son was a rich man's heir. Charles Darwin had already begun to question whether he even needed to work at all.

SELECTION
The young Darwin was unaware that he was already "selecting" a career path for himself. His failure at Latin and Greek closed off any chance of studying law, while his poor mathematical ability would make it impossible for him to study natural philosophy.

Even as Darwin busied himself in shooting and chemistry, his father had realized that medicine was the only course of study left to him at which he stood any chance of succeeding.

The Disgrace

DARWIN'S LACK OF PROGRESS AT SCHOOL, AND HIS DOGGED INTEREST IN SCIENCE, PERSUADED HIS FATHER TO SET HIM UP AS A MEDICAL APPRENTICE, AND THEN TO ORDER HIM AWAY TO STUDY MEDICINE AT UNIVERSITY. HOWEVER, DARWIN NEGLECTED HIS STUDIES—A DECISION HE WOULD LATER COME TO REGRET.

Darwin's father was a legendarily good judge of character, and attributed some of his powers to his ability to determine someone's personality from examining the shape of their head and their physiognomy. Darwin offered several accounts of his father's abilities, and in most cases tied them to lateral thinking and meticulous observation. When on a call, Robert Darwin would observe not only his patients' ailments, but also their living arrangements, possessions, and habits, in search of clues to problems that might not be explained through traditional means.

For everything else, there was phrenology, a contemporary fad for observing the bumps on someone's head, or the size and shape of their facial features, in order to search for clues about their supposed characteristics.

Unfortunately for Darwin, his father had come to suspect that the shapes of his youngest son's face revealed a boy who risked a life of idleness and dissipation. Despite multiple testimonies from other family members that Darwin's father was immensely proud of him in later life, Darwin's own memories of his father are dominated by the image of Robert Darwin telling him: "You care for nothing but shooting, dogs, and rat-catching, and you will be a disgrace to yourself and all your family!"

The Black Sheep

Darwin's father believed to some extent in a family curse—a predisposition among the Darwins either to aspire to greatness or fail spectacularly. Grandfather Erasmus might have been a man of letters, but not all of his offspring aspired to such greatness. One of Darwin's uncles, the Charles after whom

MIND SCIENCE
Phrenologists believed that the shape of a skull could provide clues as to the nature of the brain beneath it. It usually came with the implication that characteristics were locked in at birth—that royalty were born with the brains of rulers, intellectuals' intelligence was predetermined, and that criminals were predisposed to offend.

he was named, had died as a 19-year-old medical student in Edinburgh, having contracted an infection from a diseased brain he had dissected. Another uncle, another Erasmus, committed suicide by throwing himself into the river at the bottom of his garden. Two more relatives, an uncle and aunt, died in infancy, and Darwin's maternal uncle, Thomas Wedgwood, had died from opium addiction in 1805. Although not an issue at the time, there was also a history of intestinal upsets among the Wedgwoods, which Darwin would later appear to have inherited through his frail mother Susannah.

With Erasmus away at university, Darwin's father began to look less tolerantly at his younger son's behavior, and instead suspected that Charles might become another addition to the family's growing flock of black sheep.

In farming communities without full-time rat catchers, the carcass of a dead rat would fetch two pence. Rat catching was an "honest profession" in the eyes of farmers, but no way for a gentleman's son to earn a living.

The Apprentice

Darwin finished school for good in June 1825, allowed to quit Dr. Butler's curriculum by a father who understood that he was learning nothing there. Instead, the 16-year-old was made to spend the summer accompanying his father on medical rounds. Darwin took great pleasure in visiting some of Robert's minor patients, listening to their complaints, and then reporting back—this was a relatively harmless occupation, allowing Darwin to speculate without risk about the cures, putting him in the presence of grateful clients, and indulging his love of note-taking and classifying. He took less relish in the news from Erasmus of what other jobs awaited a young doctor: the clearance of blood and pus, the stench of disease, and the dissection of cadavers.

Robert had decided to send Darwin away to Edinburgh University, the third generation of Darwins to study at the institution. However, it wasn't just family tradition that shaped his decision, Edinburgh was a finely appointed and modern medical school, arguably better than Cambridge. Most importantly, Erasmus was about to head to Edinburgh for studies of his own—the elder brother would be expected to watch over his wayward younger sibling.

"I wrote down as full an account as I could of the cases with all the symptoms, and read them aloud to my father, who suggested further enquiries, and advised me what medicines to give, which I made up myself."

CHAPTER TWO

EDINBURGH AND CAMBRIDGE

The Dissenters' Sanctuary

DARWIN ARRIVED AT EDINBURGH UNIVERSITY AT A TIME OF RELIGIOUS AND EDUCATIONAL CONTROVERSY. EDINBURGH WAS THE FINEST PLACE IN THE BRITISH ISLES TO STUDY MEDICINE, BUT WAS SPLIT BY INTERNAL RIVALRIES. DARWIN HAD MIXED FEELINGS ABOUT THE VARIABLE QUALITY OF HIS TEACHERS, AND HIS INITIAL FERVOR SOON TURNED TO IDLENESS ONCE MORE.

Edinburgh University, across the border in Scotland, did not require students to pledge allegiance to the Thirty-Nine Articles of the Church of England. Cambridge University, however, would not admit a student who did not swear he believed in the Holy Trinity, the resurrection of Christ, the truth of the Old Testament and its non-contradiction of the New Testament, and numerous other articles of faith. To Unitarians such as the Darwins, such ideas were contrary to the beliefs of many members of the family. More importantly for a young scientist in the early 19th century, the Articles were a barrier to academic learning. As chemistry broke down the component parts of life, medicine offered cures that earlier ages might have found miraculous, and geology began to question the age of the Earth, the insistence on the Articles had left some universities south of the border lagging far behind the progress of Edinburgh. Meanwhile, students at Edinburgh enjoyed strong contacts with the European mainland, and access to a wealth of modern European ideas.

Teachers and Taught

Despite Edinburgh's enlightened reputation, the quality of teaching was variable. Many of the professors were appointed for political, rather than meritocratic reasons. Since funding relied largely on student numbers, the better professors supposedly attracted the largest classes.

Darwin was one of 900 new arrivals at the medical school that year, one of over 200 Englishmen who had come to sample the better standard of teaching. Darwin was unimpressed with many of the lecturers. Andrew Duncan, the son of the man who had attended to the funeral of the last Darwin boy to study in Edinburgh, was written off as "so very learned that his wisdom has left little room for his sense."

One of the main buildings of Edinburgh University, already a solid edifice of British learning by 1827.

LIFE SKILLS

Perhaps the most useful skill that Darwin picked up in Edinburgh was taxidermy, which he learned in a series of classes taught on Lothian Street by John Edmonstone. Edmonstone was a freed African slave, who had learned how to stuff animals in Guyana. Edmonstone also had many stories to tell of the life and animals of South America, and may have inspired Darwin to make a trip there himself.

"I am going to learn to stuff birds, from a blackamoor ... he only charges one guinea, for an hour every day for two months."

The Strontium Doc

Darwin's one true love was the "chemical dramas" offered by Thomas Charles Hope, the scientist who had discovered a new element in the Scottish town of Strontian—naming Strontium in the place's honor. Hope's chemistry lectures were always packed with eager scientists, adoring ladies, and simple gawpers. Many onlookers were simply waiting in hope for something to go spectacularly and entertainingly wrong in Hope's idiosyncratic experiments.

Hope was such a good showman and educator that he lived solely off the fees from teaching, and Darwin liked "both him & his lectures very much."

The Sight of Blood

Unfortunately for Darwin, the only elements he truly could not stand were those appertaining directly to a medical education. Darwin was revolted by the sight of dissection, and sickened by the operations that he witnessed, which were carried out before the invention of anesthetic. He saw "two very bad operations, one on a child, but I rushed away before they were completed."

In later life, however, he would berate himself for not persevering. An older, wiser Darwin was sure that, given time, he would have overcome his queasiness—as all doctors must. Instead, he began to fall behind in his medical studies, as both he and Erasmus still clung to the notion that they were the sons of a country squire, and would never really have to do any real work.

"I became convinced from various small circumstances," confessed Darwin, "that my father would leave me property enough to subsist on with some comfort ... my belief was sufficient to check any strenuous effort to learn medicine."

North of the border, the University of Edinburgh was free from the restrictions imposed by the Thirty-Nine Articles of the Church of England, and was a more modern institution than its English counterparts.

The Northern Athens

THE GHOULISH AND OVER-CROWDED ANATOMY LECTURES, COUPLED WITH THEIR NOT SO SECRET CONNECTIONS TO THE EDINBURGH UNDERWORLD, SOON PUT DARWIN OFF. IN HIS SECOND YEAR AT EDINBURGH, HE JOINED A STUDENT SCIENCE CLUB, WHICH PRESENTED HIM WITH INSPIRATIONS AND IDEAS FAR BEYOND THOSE IN THE COURSES HE WAS STUDYING.

Human anatomy was the most vital course of study for any would-be physician, but Darwin was deeply unimpressed with the lectures of Alexander Monro, who would drone from a podium while a demonstrator (or "prosecutor," in the language of the university) dissected a cadaver nearby. The students were ranged in a series of tiers, peering down on the display, and often too far away to see much of any use.

Dr. Monro, complained Darwin, "made his lectures on human anatomy as dull as he was himself, and the subject disgusted me."

The Resurrectionists

The medical colleges in Edinburgh were unable to offer better facilities because they suffered from a drastic shortage of dead bodies on which to practice. Surgeons were only allowed to dissect the corpses of convicted, executed murderers. And, with only a few dozen being hanged each year, the supply of murderers soon ran out—particularly since there was no means of refrigerating a corpse, and the bodies would soon decompose.

Grave-robbing—stealing the jewelry or personal items from a coffin—was a considered a serious crime. However, somewhat counterintuitively, stealing the body itself was only a misdemeanor and carried relatively light penalties, leading a new group of entrepreneurs, the "body-snatchers" or "resurrectionists," to sneak into graveyards, steal freshly buried corpses, and sell them on to academics who were prepared to keep questions to a minimum.

The risk of body-snatching became so great, particularly in the light of the rising demand of the Edinburgh surgeons' college, that relatives would keep vigils over new graves, pay guards to stay in nearby watchtowers, or authorize the construction of iron cages or "mortsafes" to keep would-be grave robbers out. Even Darwin's namesake uncle, who had died in Edinburgh, had been entombed in a strongly fortified grave to deter just such a raid.

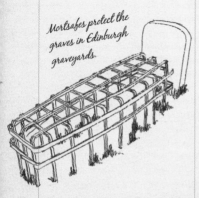

Mortsafes protect the graves in Edinburgh graveyards.

BURKE AND HARE

In 1827, the year that Darwin left Edinburgh, the body-snatching craze reached its ghoulishly logical conclusion. The Irish criminals William Burke and William Hare began supplying the colleges by murdering fresh victims, bypassing the cemeteries altogether. After the pair were caught, the government passed the Anatomy Act of 1832, which had the effect of increasing the legal availability of cadavers to the medical profession.

The Plinian Society

Darwin spent his summer on a walking tour in North Wales, culminating in an ascent of Mount Snowdon. He went riding with his elder sister Caroline, and returned to Shrewsbury in the autumn. He spent many happy days shooting with the Wedgwoods, and became firm friends with his mother's brother, Josiah Wedgwood II, or "Uncle Jos," a "silent and reserved man" whom Darwin deeply respected for his sense of righteousness.

Back in Edinburgh without Erasmus, Darwin was lured away from human medicine by the Plinian Society, a club that "consisted of students and met in an underground room in the university for the sake of reading papers on natural science and discussing them."

"I listened in silent astonishment, and as far as I can judge, without any effect on my mind."

Robert Edmond Grant

Darwin met Robert Grant (1793–1874), a biologist who would take him on long walks along the nearby beaches. It was through Grant that Darwin's name first got into print, when Darwin made two minor discoveries in marine biology. He had noticed that the larvae of the coral-like bryozoan *Flustra* (or "sea-mat") had tiny moving hairs, or *cilia*, that allowed them to swim freely. He also deduced that the black dots often found in oyster shells were actually the eggs of a parasite, the skate leech. Darwin reported both of these discoveries to Grant, and was somewhat taken aback when Grant published the "discovery" as his own. Although Darwin presented his findings in person at a public meeting a few days later, and Grant acknowledged him in a footnote, the experience left him permanently wary of the early disclosure of his scientific discoveries.

Bryozoans and "sea-mats" as cataloged by the German biologist Ernst Haeckel (see p. 146).

Lamarck's Heresy

On one of their walks, Grant confided in Darwin that he believed in the theories of the French scientist Jean-Baptiste Lamarck (1744–1829), who had suggested that higher life forms had somehow been created through the transformation over many generations of lower life forms. The idea that life had "evolved"—a term used by Grant's friend Robert Jameson in an anonymous paper of 1826—was a great shock to Darwin. Even though it mirrored his grandfather's own theories, it suggested that life on Earth had not been put there by God, but had arisen without Him.

"My summer vacations during these two years were wholly given up to amusements."

Neptune and Pluto

ANOTHER CONTROVERSY AT
EDINBURGH RAGED, NOT
ONLY BETWEEN DISCIPLINES
BUT BETWEEN LECTURERS, AS
TWO OF DARWIN'S MENTORS
DUELLED OVER GEOLOGICAL
ISSUES. ALTHOUGH DARWIN
CLAIMED THAT THE FEUD LEFT
HIM WITH LITTLE INTEREST
IN ROCKS AND STRATA, HE
LEARNED ENOUGH TO PUT
THIS KNOWLEDGE TO GOOD
USE IN THE ESTABLISHMENT
OF HIS OWN THEORIES AS A
MATURE SCIENTIST.

In the early 19th century, William Smith (1769–1839) produced a geological map of Britain, identifying the various types and ages of rock. He helped create the science of stratigraphy (the study of the origin, composition, and distribution of strata), as geologists rushed to compare layers elsewhere, arguing over the relative positions of rocks to create a record of earlier ages.

Neptunism and Plutonism

The German geologist Abraham Werner (1749–1817) argued that the different layers of rocks were evidence that a great ocean had once covered the entire Earth. Sediment and precipitation from this ocean had formed different layers on its seabed, and over billions of years, this sediment had formed different kinds of rocks. Because of its claims of a marine origin, Werner's theory was named Neptunism, after the Roman god of the sea.

However, Werner's theory was criticized because it failed to explain why this world-ocean had receded. Moreover, the massive amount of time that would have been required for it to do so stood at odds with the Bible's creation story, and the relatively young Earth that it implied.

Another problem with Werner's theory was the presence of basalts, which did not necessarily form in conveniently horizontal plates ("sills") on the ground, but in intrusive sheets between other strata, or even in vertical columns or "dikes."

A solution to this was offered by Plutonism, which took its name from the Roman god of the underworld. James Hutton (1726–97), a leading Plutonist who is considered by many to have been the father of modern geology, suggested that the Earth had once been a mass of molten rock that had slowly cooled, creating the different strata as it did so. Since volcanoes were known to produce lava, and lava cooled to produce a kind of rock, it was surely more sensible to suggest that the dikes and sills of the stratigraphical record had been produced by the action of forces from beneath the Earth's surface.

Abraham Werner was Inspector and Teacher of Mining and Mineralogy at the University of Leipzig. He attracted students from all over Europe and was inducted into the Swedish Academy of Sciences.

Terrible Lizards

Darwin stumbled into geology at a time when scientists had begun to appreciate the role that fossils could play in helping to identify the age of rocks. The French naturalist Georges Cuvier (1769–1832) conducted a stratigraphical survey of the region around Paris, and noted in the process that particular types of fossil persisted in the same kind of rock, albeit in different locations. Cuvier's discovery not only encouraged other geologists to use similar tactics, but also ignited debate on dominant life forms. Cuvier noted that the fossil record suggested that there had been a time when reptiles, not mammals, ruled the Earth. He even began cataloging some of the larger specimens—creatures that would, in 1842, be named "dinosaurs" by the British scientist Richard Owen.

Three small ammonite fossils, each approximately 3/5 in (1.5 cm) across.

> *"The sole effect they produced on me was the determination never as long as I lived to read a book on Geology or in any way to study the science."*

Jameson vs. Hope

Darwin's favorite lecturer, Thomas Hope, was a friend of Hutton, and it was no surprise either that he would be a Plutonist, or that Darwin would favor the Plutonist argument. However, not everyone agreed, and Hope would duel constantly with another of Darwin's lecturers, Robert Jameson (1774–1854), much to their students' glee.

"Dr. Hope is decidedly opposed to me," said Jameson, "and I am opposed to Dr. Hope, and between us we make the subject interesting."

Darwin, however, disagreed: "During my second year at Edinburgh," wrote Darwin, "I attended Professor Jameson's lectures on Geology and Zoology, but they were incredibly dull." Darwin's surviving college textbooks bear witness to his boredom—he and a classmate seem to have had greater fun writing on Jameson's *Manual of Mineralogy* in class, inventing great honors for themselves, writing snide comments, and doodling.

Unlike Hope, Jameson was a Neptunist, and also had a habit of ridiculing rival theories, which some students enjoyed, but of which Darwin disapproved. Darwin recalled that he once "heard Professor Jameson, in a field lecture at Salisbury Craigs, discoursing on a trap-dyke ... with volcanic rocks all around us, and say that it was a fissure filled with sediment from above, adding with a sneer that there were men who maintained that it had been injected from below in a molten condition." Darwin remained shocked at his own memory, not that Jameson had been so ungentlemanly, but that the assumption that volcanic rocks were not volcanic had still held sway within his own living memory.

SNAKE STONES

Ammonites are an extinct family of marine creatures believed to have resembled squid. They flourished between 400 and 65 million years ago, and hence can be found in many parts of the fossil record.

In places where there was no life on the sea floor, ammonite shells are often the only fossils to be found, dropping to the sea floor after a life spent floating above it.

In medieval times, ammonites were believed to be snakes turned into stone by saints. In the classical era, they were referred to as "Horns of Ammon," for their resemblance to the ram's horns on the god Zeus Ammon, from which their modern name is derived.

A Country Parson?

WHEN IT BECAME CLEAR
THAT DARWIN WAS NOT CUT
OUT FOR A MEDICAL CAREER,
HIS FATHER RECALLED HIM
FROM EDINBURGH. ROBERT
DARWIN DECIDED HIS
WAYWARD SON SHOULD EARN
AN HONEST DEGREE, BECOME
AN ANGLICAN VICAR, AND LIVE
OUT HIS DAYS AS A COUNTRY
PARSON.

None of Darwin's geological or zoological education would be much use to him as a doctor, a fact that eventually came to Robert Darwin's attention.

"After having spent two sessions in Edinburgh, my father perceived or he heard from my sisters, that I did not like the thought of being a physician, so he proposed that I should become a clergyman."

Darwin took his time deciding. He accompanied Uncle Jos on a brief trip to Paris, the only time in his life he would visit Europe. He wandered around tourist sights with a few college friends while Jos picked up two of his daughters from Switzerland, where they had been studying. Darwin then returned with Jos and the girls, 21-year-old Fanny and 19-year-old Emma. Although Darwin did not know it at the time, the latter was to become his wife over a decade later.

Articles of Faith

Darwin was obliged to read through several books on the Anglican faith, in order to determine that he could bring himself to swear to the Thirty-Nine Articles of the Church of England, without which he would not be admitted to Cambridge University. Although Darwin did not understand everything he read, he found nothing with which he really felt much like arguing, and even began to look forward to a sleepy rural church—he was already thinking, as was his father, that hunting and fishing would keep him as busy as his religious duties.

"It never struck me," he wrote, "how illogical it was to say I believed in what I could not understand and what is in fact unintelligible."

"I did not then in the least doubt the strict and literal truth of every word in the Bible."

Christ's College

Darwin arrived too late at Christ's College, Cambridge, to be accepted during the Easter term. Obliged to wait until the autumn, he took lodgings above a tobacconist. His studies began in earnest late in 1828, although Darwin's heart did not really seem to be in it. He attended lectures and compulsory daily trips to the chapel, and secretly spent an allowance from his sisters and father on a new gun.

Darwin eventually passed his examinations, without any great fanfare, and spent his last two terms at Cambridge in

Darwin had modest rooms at Christ's College, which were restored to their original state and opened to the public as part of the centenary celebrations of *On the Origin of Species*.

1831, secure in the knowledge that he was already a Bachelor of Arts. A master's degree should (and would) follow without undue effort, after which Darwin could expect to take theological orders and finally put his father's mind to rest about his career choice.

But while his letters home continued to give the impression of an uninterested but plodding clergyman in waiting, his daily life in Cambridge still bore elements of his old interests. Despite his lack of interest in most forms of education, he would dedicate hours to toying with his gun. He would practice shouldering it in the mirror, to ensure that he got the best angles at once; and even experiment for hours with a firing cap loaded, using the puff of air it generated to blow out a candle. One of his tutors, hearing only the noise, assumed that Darwin spent day after day in his room, cracking a horse whip for no apparent reason.

However, shooting and hunting were not unusual occupations for the more idle residents of Cambridge, who had no desire to study until absolutely necessary. Darwin, though, had developed a new interest, one that kept him occupied throughout the holidays and often during term-time. His distant cousin, William Darwin Fox, with whom Darwin spent much of his time, shared this passion. "I am dying by inches," Darwin griped in a letter to Fox during one vacation, "from not having any body to talk to about insects." Darwin was crazy about bugs.

"Considering how fiercely I have been attacked by the orthodox, it seems ludicrous that I once intended to be a clergyman."

Beetles and Rocks

EVEN AS A CLERGYMAN IN TRAINING, DARWIN WAS UNABLE TO TEAR HIMSELF AWAY FROM HIS PURSUIT OF THE NATURAL SCIENCES. HE FELL IN WITH A CONTEMPORARY FAD FOR ENTOMOLOGY, AND ALSO BEFRIENDED JOHN HENSLOW, A DON WITH AN INTEREST IN MINERALOGY AND BOTANY, AND A MAN WHO WOULD CHANGE DARWIN'S LIFE FOREVER.

"No pursuit at Cambridge," wrote Darwin, "was followed with nearly so much eagerness or gave me so much pleasure as collecting beetles... No poet ever felt more delight at seeing his first poem published than I did at seeing in *Stephens' Illustrations of British Insects* the magic words 'captured by C. Darwin, Esq.'"

Darwin and Fox would wander the countryside with their dogs, determined to find rare insects. Most, they would simply capture, mount on cardboard, and compare against the tables in a collector's book. Sometimes, they would find something rare or apparently undiscovered, and swooped upon the opportunity for their names to appear, however briefly, in the rolls of honor of fellow entomologists.

"I will give proof of my zeal," Darwin wrote in his memoirs. "One day, on tearing off some old bark, I saw two rare beetles and seized one in each hand; then I saw a third and new kind, which I could not bear to lose, so that I popped the one that I held in my right hand into my mouth. Alas, it injected some intensely acrid fluid, which burnt my tongue so that I was forced to spit the beetle out, which was lost, as well as the third one."

Darwin became such a keen beetle hunter that he even hired an assistant, paying a local man to collect the debris from the bottom of the barges that brought reeds from the nearby fens, and thereby stole a march on his many competitors. Whereas they went to the fens looking for new discoveries, Darwin had the fens brought to him.

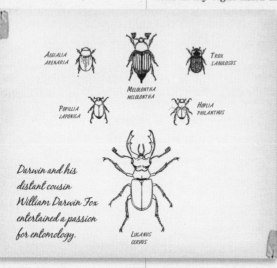

AEGIALIA ARENARIA

MELOLONTHA MELOLONTHA

TROX SABULOSUS

POPILLIA JAPONICA

HOPLIA PHILANTHUS

LUCANUS CERVUS

Darwin and his distant cousin William Darwin Fox entertained a passion for entomology.

"The three years which I spent at Cambridge were the most joyful in my happy life."

Walking with Henslow

However, beetles weren't Darwin's only inspiration. At long last, he finally found a tutor who truly stirred him. John Steyens Henslow (1796–1861) was only a few years older than Darwin, and appeared to be following a similar career path. He had already been a professor of mineralogy and botany, but was preparing to put aside both disciplines in order to become a country parson.

Darwin spent so much time with his new mentor that the other dons began to refer to him as "the man who walks with Henslow." The admiration was mutual, and Henslow found in Darwin an eager and inquisitive pupil, sure to enliven lectures with pertinent questions. Darwin was often asked to assist at Henslow's demonstrations, and accompanied Henslow on field trips in the environs of Cambridge.

Through Henslow, Darwin met Adam Sedgwick (1785–1873), a prominent Cambridge geologist. Sedgwick took Darwin on a field trip to Wales, staying at the Mount in Shrewsbury en route, where he amazed Darwin's sisters with his academic erudition—although Robert Darwin, it must be said, was somewhat less impressed.

On the trip, the two men advanced along the Vale of Clwyd looking for interesting items where a world of limestone met a world of red sandstone. Sedgwick also took Darwin to caves where the fossils of rhinoceroses had been found—a real mystery for early Victorian scientists to solve. On the way home, Darwin parted ways with Sedgwick, although he made sure he was back in time for a partridge shoot.

Help Wanted

Back in late August 1831 after a shooting trip with Uncle Jos, Darwin found a letter from Henslow. It informed him of an odd opportunity to travel to Tierra del Fuego (the "Land of Fire") at the very tip of South America, and then home again via the East Indies, aboard a Royal Naval vessel whose captain required a companion to provide company on the long voyage. The post would suit anyone with an interest in natural science and who had no other responsibilities. The successful applicant would have little to do except search for new plant and animal species, or observe the geology and botany of distant places.

Henslow suggested that it would be an ideal way for Darwin to stretch his investigative legs, before settling down as a country parson. If he wanted the post, he should not delay. The ship would sail in just a few weeks. Her name was the *Beagle*.

FOSSILS AND FERTILIZER

Even after becoming a country parson, Henslow appointed an underling to hold most services, and remained a professor of botany at Cambridge.

He often meddled in the affairs of local farmers with new suggestions; and it was Henslow who noticed that coprolites (fossilized animal feces) worked as a powerful fertilizer, a discovery that helped create the modern industry in phosphate fertilizers.

Adam Sedgwick was an early colleague of Darwin, but would savagely oppose his theory of natural selection in later life, calling it "utterly false."

The Chance of a Lifetime

A CALAMITY IN THE SOUTH ATLANTIC BROUGHT A UNIQUE OPPORTUNITY TO DARWIN: THE OFFER OF A PLACE ON A TWO-YEAR SOUTH AMERICAN SURVEY, AS A NATURALIST ABOARD HMS *BEAGLE*. IT WAS SURE TO MAKE HIS NAME, BUT FIRST HE NEEDED TO PERSUADE HIS DOUBTFUL FATHER.

The job was a bizarre one. Robert FitzRoy (1805–63), the newly appointed captain of HMS *Beagle*, had made it known that he would like a "gentleman" to accompany him on the ship's next round-the-world survey. The voyage was expected to last two years or more, and the likely candidate would need to share a cramped cabin with junior officers. Crucially, the passenger would not be a member of the crew. He would be expected to pay his own way, and the mission would be best suited to someone with an artistic or scientific interest who wanted to see the world.

Suicide Risk

FitzRoy's reason for his request was rooted in tragedy. Three years earlier, the *Beagle*'s former captain Pringle Stokes had taken his own life in Tierra del Fuego, driven mad by his useless charts, his ailing crew, and the miserable weather. "The soul of man dies in him," he had written in his logbook. Then he shot himself.

Robert FitzRoy, a naval man with a dark family secret that he hoped to fight with Darwin's help.

His replacement, Robert FitzRoy, was a well-connected aristocrat, independently wealthy and blessed with a meteoric rise in the Royal Navy. But he also had a family history of suicide, and fretted that he, too, would slide into fatal depression if he had nobody to talk to on the *Beagle*'s next voyage.

As no captain could allow himself to become friendly with his crew, what FitzRoy needed was a traveling companion who could keep him sane. The man would need to be a gentleman, of course, of good family, with an interest in science, who would regard a minimum of two years in a tiny survey ship as an adventure and not a prison sentence.

"The Very Man"

FitzRoy's idea had drifted through the Cambridge network. Henslow considered it himself, but with a wife and young child, as well as his daily affairs, he could not spare the time. Henslow passed the offer to Leonard Jenyns, a younger parson, but Jenyns could not bring himself to give up his new posting. The ideal candidate, Henslow realized, would be someone who had no other prospects; a man with a scientific mind but no troublesome responsibilities to tie him down, whether marital, theological, or otherwise.

"Don't put on any modest doubts or fears about your disqualifications," Henslow urged Darwin, "for I assure you I think you are the very man they are in search of."

Darwin accepted immediately, only for his father to stamp on the idea as dangerous, pointless, and counter-productive. "If you can find any man of common sense who advises you to go," said Robert, "I will give my consent."

Darwin immediately left for Maer Hall, ostensibly to go shooting again with Uncle Jos. But, in fact, he knew that Josiah Wedgwood II was the very man to talk Robert Darwin around, and presented his uncle with a list of his father's objections. On September 1, 1831, Darwin wrote to his father, begging him to change his mind.

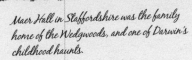

Maer Hall in Staffordshire was the family home of the Wedgwoods, and one of Darwin's childhood haunts.

With his own letter, Darwin enclosed Uncle Jos's comments. Wedgwood thought it was entirely in character for clergymen to study natural history; he trusted the Admiralty to send a ship suitable for the task, and he noted that since Charles was doing nothing else, it was hardly a great loss. Wedgwood thought two years aboard the *Beagle* was sure to be at least as useful in Darwin's education as two more years in England.

Much to Darwin's surprise, those letters alone were enough to change his father's mind. With Robert Darwin's blessing, Charles began to make hasty preparations for the voyage of the *Beagle*.

I have given Uncle Jos what I fervently trust is an accurate and full list of your objections, and he is kind enough to give his opinion on all.

- Disreputable to my character as a Clergyman hereafter
- A wild scheme
- That they must have offered to many others before me the place of Naturalist
- And from its not being accepted there must be some serious objection to the vessel or expedition
- That I should never settle down to a steady life hereafter
- That my accommodations would be most uncomfortable
- That you should consider it as again changing my profession
- That it would be a useless undertaking

— CHARLES DARWIN TO HIS FATHER, 1831

Doubts and Delays

TO DARWIN'S INTENSE FRUSTRATION, HIS PLACE ABOARD THE *BEAGLE* WAS NOT GUARANTEED, AS HE HAD BEEN LED TO BELIEVE IT WOULD BE. EVEN AFTER HIS BERTH WAS SECURE, THE SHIP WAS SUBJECT TO MISHAPS, BAD WEATHER, AND TECHNICAL PROBLEMS THAT DELAYED ITS SAILING FOR SEVERAL WEEKS.

Darwin rushed to Cambridge to discuss his mission with Henslow, extravagantly hiring a private coach to take him the last part of the journey. It was only then that an embarrassed letter arrived from FitzRoy, suggesting that the Cambridge clique had misread his intentions. Yes, he wrote, he wanted a gentleman companion, but not some stranger appointed by dons. He rather hoped to bring along a friend of his instead, and so the position was already practically filled. His hopes dashed, Darwin was ready to give up on the idea.

Darwin arrived back in London three days ahead of the coronation of William IV, and somewhat despondently paid a courtesy call on FitzRoy. But waiting for him was another surprise. Before Darwin could even exchange pleasantries, FitzRoy revealed that his preferred choice, a personal friend, had backed out, and the place was Darwin's if he wanted it.

Making Plans

In town for the coronation, Darwin allowed himself to squander a whole guinea on a good seat to watch the procession. For the rest of the week, he accompanied the extravagantly wealthy FitzRoy on shopping expeditions for supplies: buying barometers, books, and a series of firearms to deal with surly

HMS *Beagle* was a ten-gun *Cherokee*-class brig sloop, though its armaments had been reduced to six guns by the time Darwin came aboard.

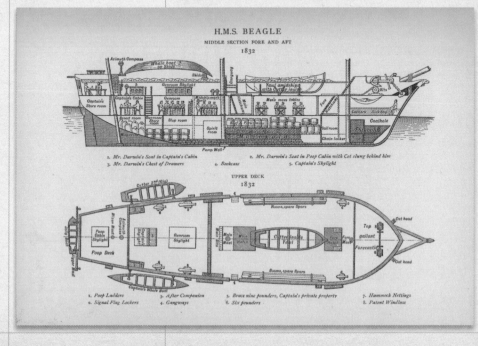

H.M.S. BEAGLE
MIDDLE SECTION FORE AND AFT
1832

1. *Mr. Darwin's Seat in Captain's Cabin*   2. *Mr. Darwin's Seat in Poop Cabin with Cot slung behind him*
3. *Mr. Darwin's Chest of Drawers*   4. *Bookcase*   5. *Captain's Skylight*

UPPER DECK
1832

1. *Poop Ladders*   3. *After Companion*   5. *Brass nine pounders, Captain's private property*   7. *Hammock Nettings*
2. *Signal Flag Lockers*   4. *Gangways*   6. *Six pounders*   8. *Patent Windlass*

natives. He also established another crucial fact—since he was not in the employment of the Royal Navy, his scientific specimens would technically belong to him. This matter of ownership would be a vital factor in establishing Darwin as an independent researcher, and afford him access to his collection, whereas an officer might have been forced to hand it over to higher authorities.

"You can have no idea how busy I am all day long.—& owing to my confidence in Cap Fitzroy I am as happy as a king."

On September 11, FitzRoy took Darwin to see the ship herself, cunningly forcing him to take a steamboat from London along the Kent coast, instead of the shorter, more direct route overland to Plymouth. Darwin's pronouncement that he "scarcely ever spent three pleasanter days" was enough to persuade FitzRoy (falsely, as it would turn out) that Darwin would not be troubled by seasickness.

The *Beagle* at Last

Darwin was not prepared for the small size of the *Beagle*, recalling his father's doubts that the ship was too small to reasonably attempt a global voyage. The *Beagle*'s crewmen sized up the new arrival in quite another fashion. Darwin reported that Lieutenant John Clements Wickham "grumbled merely at the number of my natural cubic inches," leading Darwin to fret that he would be even less welcome when he returned with his bulky luggage. The *Beagle* was an aging, cramped ship, and what few luxuries she had were being installed at FitzRoy's personal expense.

The Beagle had a crew of 65, as well as nine passengers including Darwin.

Darwin had expected to leave England in October, but the *Beagle* was delayed in port for another ten weeks. Kicking his heels, he suffered from nervous heart palpitations; was teased by the idle officers with tall tales of foreign climes; and was left to "try and look as much like a sailor as ever I can," admitting himself that he fooled nobody. By October 24, the next cancelled sailing date, Darwin had begun to keep a diary. At first it was dull and pedestrian, but soon Darwin embellished it with ever more detailed notes on characters, phenomena, and events.

All the while, he continued to worry about the ship's tiny proportions, particularly when other travelers began to arrive with their own luggage. "The absolute want of room," he wrote, "is an evil, that nothing can surmount." While the *Beagle* continued to sit at anchor, the dreary British autumn gave way to winter, complete with drizzle, cold winds, and further worries.

A MACABRE REMINDER
On November 21, one of the *Beagle*'s sailors fell overboard and drowned. The news was deeply shocking to Darwin, reminding him that if such disasters could befall the crew before the ship had even left port, the danger on the open sea would be even greater.

"These two months at Plymouth were the most miserable that I ever spent."

ABOARD
THE
BEAGLE

Passengers and Crew

"He is no loss."

— DARWIN ON MCCORMICK'S
DEPARTURE

Artist Conrad Martens, whose
dinner was once dragged off by
Darwin as a scientific
specimen.

As Darwin had already begun to observe in his diary, he was far from being the only person of interest aboard the *Beagle* for its momentous voyage:

John Clements Wickham (1798–64), lieutenant aboard the *Beagle* on her second voyage, soon altered his view of Darwin as a literal waste of space. After the ship returned to England, he would take over as captain, and take her on another voyage.

Lieutenant John Lort Stokes (1812–85) monitored the 24 clocks aboard the *Beagle*. One of the mission's objectives was to use the difference between local time and Greenwich Mean Time to determine the longitude of various foreign locations, to aid later vessels in navigation. He would also later become a captain of the *Beagle*, taking over from Wickham, and eventually rose to the rank of admiral.

Lieutenant Bartholomew Sulivan (1810–90) was a surveyor, whose job was to map coastal waters. He would later put the same training to use in the Falklands and during the Crimean War, when he found suitable waters for the Royal Navy to conduct attacks in the Baltic. For his service to the Crown, he was made a vice-admiral and knighted in 1869.

Syms Covington (1816–61) was a teenager. Originally hired as a "fiddler and cabin boy," Covington was soon employed by Darwin as his full-time assistant, collecting samples, cataloging collections, and even shooting some of the animals. He would remain in Darwin's service for several years before emigrating to Australia in 1839. Even then, he was prevailed upon to send his old shipmate Australian barnacles by post.

Philip Gidley King (1817–1904) was a teenage midshipman, and the scion of a famous naval family. His namesake grandfather had been the founder of the first European settlement on Norfolk Island, east of Australia, and his father, Philip Parker King, had been a former captain of the *Beagle*. Born in Australia, King the younger had been encouraged to draw and paint, but admitted his skills were lacking. He would return to Australia after the *Beagle* voyage.

Short-Term Companions

The artist Augustus Earle (1793–1838) was commissioned to record the Beagle's greatest moments, but succumbed to ill health and was let off the ship in Brazil. His replacement, Conrad Martens (1801–78) stayed with the ship for half the voyage, and once famously shot, cooked, and partly ate a local bird before Darwin realized it was a previously uncataloged species and stole the rest of his dinner.

By paying his way onto the ship, Darwin had inadvertently trodden on the toes of the ship's surgeon, Robert

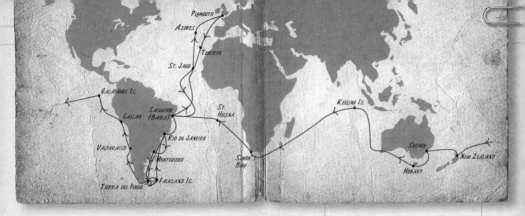

McCormick, an irascible man who resented Darwin's "gentle-man" status—the surgeon was not allowed to dine with the captain. More importantly, a ship's surgeon was widely under-stood in the Royal Navy to be the designated naturalist on any voyage, and McCormick had hoped to make a name for himself by publishing his own findings on the ship's return. Instead, he soon grew frustrated with Darwin's enthusiasm and dedica-tion, and jealous of the free time Darwin had to pursue exactly the sort of enquiries McCormick would have liked to make him-self. McCormick would storm off the *Beagle* in Brazil, claiming that he "found myself in a false position on board a small and very uncomfortable vessel, and very much disappointed in my expectations of carrying out my natural history pursuits…"

The Fuegians

Strangest of all the travelers aboard the *Beagle*, at least to British eyes, were three natives from Tierra del Fuego. In 1830, FitzRoy had got into a fight on the remotest tip of South America with some natives who had tried to steal his boats. He had taken four prisoners (one died later), and rashly decided to bring them back to England to show them the ways of civiliza-tion. He was now determined to return them to their home country, in the company of a Christian missionary.

The Fuegians comprised an adult male, York Minster (aged 27), a boy called Jemmy Button (aged 14), and a ten-year-old girl called Fuegia Basket. Having spent a year with members of the Church Mission Society, they were pronounced "civilized," to the extent that they had agreed to return to their homeland as missionaries. (Although it is difficult to see, for example, how a ten-year-old girl might have accomplished that task.) In fact, they were perhaps better described as interpreters and would-be envoys to their countrymen, accompanying a real missionary, the youthful and blithely optimistic Father Robert Matthews.

Doubts about the likely success of the Tierra del Fuego mis-sion were expressed before the *Beagle* even left port. Matthews and his native guides had arrived with crates of useless gifts from well-meaning British donors, including a complete set of china crockery, entirely unsuited to the Fuegian wilderness.

Jemmy Button

Fuegia Basket

York Minster

The three Fuegian natives whom FitzRoy considered it his duty to return to their homeland. Their names were assigned to them by the crew, who could not pronounce their real names: Orundel'lico, Yok'cushly, and El'leparu.

Crossing the Line

AFTER SOME INITIAL DOUBTS AND A BAD CASE OF SEASICKNESS THAT NEVER COMPLETELY LEFT HIM, DARWIN'S FIRST LANDFALL REJUVENATED HIS HOPES AND FILLED HIM WITH EXCITEMENT. AS THE *BEAGLE* CROSSED THE EQUATOR AND NEARED SOUTH AMERICA, NOT EVEN HIS SHAKY SEA-LEGS COULD DIM HIS ENTHUSIASM.

The *Beagle* finally set sail on the morning of December 27, 1831; and just two days out from Plymouth Darwin was sick, although it may not have been the sea that first turned his stomach. True to character, FitzRoy ordered the whipping of several crewmembers for dereliction of duty over Christmas, and Darwin was forced to listen to their screams.

Before long, Darwin admitted that it was the sea itself that was making him feel queasy. For the next week, he lay prone in his cabin, unable to eat anything but dried biscuits and raisins. In fact, it was January before he emerged on the deck, in time to see the looming volcanic peak of Tenerife—the largest of the Canary Islands in the Atlantic—in the distance.

Fear of Cholera

Faced with choppy seas, FitzRoy disregarded his plans and sailed right past Madeira. Tenerife was close enough to make similar chronometric measurements, and it would have to do.

Crew and passengers alike were eagerly awaiting dry land and winter sun. But they were thwarted by the local consul. Preceded by news of a cholera outbreak in Britain, the *Beagle* was subjected to a 12-day quarantine. When he heard of this, FitzRoy impatiently gave the order to weigh anchor, and they continued without putting ashore. Darwin was inconsolable, and rightly believed that he would never see Madeira again.

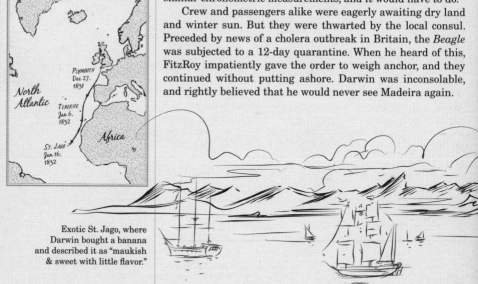

North Atlantic

PLYMOUTH
Dec 27,
1831

TENERIFE
Jan 6,
1832

ST. JAGO
Jan 16,
1832

Africa

Exotic St. Jago, where Darwin bought a banana and described it as "maukish & sweet with little flavor."

"Oh misery, misery … we have left perhaps one of the most interesting places in the world, just at the moment when we were near enough for every object to create, without satisfying, our utmost curiosity."

— DARWIN'S DIARY, JANUARY 1832

Darwin thought that he was the discoverer of the octopus's ability to change color. However, his friend Henslow had to calm his youthful zeal by informing him that this was no secret.

"My mind has been since leaving England a perfect hurricane of delight & astonishment."

— LETTER TO WILLIAM DARWIN FOX, MAY 1832

Darwin's First "Discoveries"

The *Beagle* first put ashore in the Cape Verde islands at St. Jago (now Santiago). The island was a mixture of lush, alien vegetation topped by bleak, towering volcanic peaks. FitzRoy's men began taking their measurements, leaving the ecstatic Darwin to wander for three weeks, marveling at the sight of plants and fruits he had only read about: tamarinds, bananas, and palms.

"I returned to the shore," Darwin wrote, "treading on Volcanic rocks and hearing the notes of unknown birds, and seeing new insects fluttering about the still newer flowers. It has been for me a glorious day, like giving to a blind man eyes. He is overwhelmed with what he sees and cannot justly comprehend it. Such are my feelings and such may they remain."

Darwin was inspired: amazed at the sight of an octopus changing color as it fled through the water, Darwin was convinced he had made a discovery—only for his friend Henslow to inform him later that this ability was common knowledge among zoologists.

Later, a line of seashells embedded in rock high above sea level prompted Darwin to wonder if the land had risen up more recently than other geologists supposed. "It then first dawned on me," he wrote, "that I might perhaps write a book on the geology of the various countries visited, and this made me thrill with delight. That was a memorable hour to me, and how distinctly I can call to mind the low cliff of lava beneath which I rested, with the sun glaring hot, a few strange desert plants glowing near, and with living corals in the tidal pools at my feet."

KING NEPTUNE'S CEREMONY

On February 17, 1832, Darwin came on deck to find FitzRoy incongruously dressed as King Neptune, ready to perform the mock ceremony of the Equator, which Darwin later pronounced to be "sufficiently disagreeable." Thirty-two aboard the *Beagle* had never "crossed the line" before, and were blindfolded, dunked in a water-filled sail, and made to go through a mock "shaving" by the costumed sailors.

"They then lathered my face and mouth with pitch and paint, and scraped some of it off with a piece of roughened iron hoop. A signal being given I was tilted head over heels into the water ... at last, glad enough, I escaped ... water was flying about in every direction: of course not one person, even the Captain, got clear of being wet through."

The sailors later revealed to Darwin that they had let him off lightly, because of his "high standing" on board. Darwin the outsider had finally found a group that accepted him.

Brazil

DARWIN WAS PLEASED TO MAKE LANDFALL ON THE SOUTH AMERICAN MAINLAND, BUT HIS EXCITABLE DESCRIPTIONS OF BRAZILIAN FLORA, FAUNA, AND FEMININITY HID OTHER CONCERNS. HE SUFFERED AN INFECTED WOUND, AND HAD A SERIOUS QUARREL WITH CAPTAIN FITZROY ABOUT THE ETHICS OF SLAVERY.

Darwin called Brazil a "chaos of delight." Despite an infected scratch that left him bedridden for several days, he soon took to the lush green forests with a sense of rapture, and uncovered several new species of beetles and flatworms.

However, Darwin also suffered a deep culture shock, finding himself in a society where the buying and selling of human slaves had created an environment in which anything could be similarly traded to the highest bidder. His lack of experience of foreign cultures only accentuated the difference.

Darwin immediately assumed his own superiority, and began assigning blame: "The Brazilians," he wrote, "as far as I am able to judge, possess but a small share of those qualities which give dignity to mankind. Ignorant, cowardly and indolent in the extreme ... they answer all remarks by asking 'Why cannot we do as our grandfathers before us did?'"

Masters and Servants

His arrival in South America was the first time that Darwin had come face-to-face with customs and cultures that were completely alien to him, initiating a sense of intercultural comparison that would eventually inspire some of his later works on human character.

His outrage would eventually give way to philosophical enquiry, for he was as curious about the strange development of attitudes, temperament, and character among Brazilians as he was in that of their black slaves. He noted that the presence of slaves gave the Brazilians little incentive to invest in labor-saving devices or new technologies. He was convinced, with a phrenologist's eye, that he could see "persevering cunning, sensuality and pride" stamped in the features even of priests, and that older Brazilian ladies were so used to barking orders and disciplining slaves that "they are born women, but die more like fiends." He was aghast at reports from his fellow travelers that they had seen slaves missing thumbs—the result of the use of thumbscrews by their mistresses for torture or punishment.

"It has been remarked ... that abruptly conical hills are characteristic of the formation which Humboldt designates as gneiss–granite. Nothing can be more striking than the effect of these huge rounded masses of rock rising out of the most luxuriant vegetation." — DARWIN'S DIARY, APRIL 19, 1832

"The slave in chains on supplicating knee,
Spreads his wide arms, and lifts his eye to Thee;
With hunger pale, with wounds and toil oppress'd,
'Are we not brethren?' Sorrow chokes the rest."

— Erasmus Darwin, 1791

Hot Coffee

Darwin was incensed at the plight of the slaves. Both of his grandfathers had been anti-slavery campaigners, and it was Josiah Wedgwood himself who had coined the famous slogan: "Am I not a man and a brother?"

Darwin made the mistake of raising the issue at dinner with Captain FitzRoy, who claimed that slaves were surely happy with their lot. As evidence, FitzRoy noted that he had witnessed slaves telling their master that they were happy. Darwin's terse response was noted in his diary: "I then asked him, perhaps with a sneer, whether he thought the answers of slaves in the presence of their master was worth anything. This made him excessively angry, and he said that as I doubted his word, we could not live any longer together."

Darwin had just forced FitzRoy into one of the fits of rage that the sailors who served under him had already nicknamed "hot coffee." Darwin feared he would be asked to leave the ship, but FitzRoy's tantrum soon blew over. Nevertheless Darwin was soon grateful for the chance to spend some time away from the ship. As the *Beagle* surveyed the Brazilian coast, and underwent an overhaul, Darwin hired a small cottage overlooking the idyllic Botofogo Bay, with a plain view of the majestic Corcovado mountain, an iconic symbol of modern Rio de Janeiro. However, Darwin, ever the naturalist, was more interested in its geology.

Darwin's encounter with the realities of slavery brought the anti-slavery campaigning of his grandfathers into sharp focus.

AN APRIL DOLPHIN?

Under sail on the *Beagle,* Darwin went to bed as usual on the evening of March 31, only to be woken just after midnight by Lieutenant Sulivan, asking if he had ever seen a "grampus." Thinking that Sulivan was informing him of a rare breed of dolphin, Darwin darted from his cabin onto the deck, only to be greeted by gales of laughter from the crewmen who were still awake. It was now, he realized, very early in the morning of April 1.

Tierra del Fuego

OVER THE NEXT FEW MONTHS THE *BEAGLE* VOYAGED ON DOWN THE EAST COAST OF SOUTH AMERICA, PUTTING IN AT PORTS SUCH AS BUENOS AIRES AND MONTEVIDEO. BY DECEMBER SHE HAD REACHED THE VERY TIP OF SOUTH AMERICA, AND THE WILDS OF TIERRA DEL FUEGO. IT WAS HERE THAT DARWIN OBSERVED NATIVE TRIBESMEN UP CLOSE, AND MADE AN OBSERVATION UNUSUAL FOR HIS TIME—THAT THE "SAVAGES" PERHAPS POSSESSED TALENTS THAT EUROPEANS HAD FORGOTTEN.

At the southern tip of the Americas, Darwin pronounced Tierra del Fuego as a land where "death instead of life is the predominant spirit." The climate was cold, and the natives were viewed as painted, semi-naked savages who, according to Jemmy Button, would sometimes eat their own womenfolk in winter. Father Matthews, however, shrugged off the inhospitable climate, and reiterated his desire to stay on and bring Christianity to the locals.

Strange Greetings

Although there were three Fuegians among the passengers aboard the *Beagle*, they were used to European ways. Meeting Fuegians in their own surroundings, Darwin discovered that in this part of the world, friendship was expressed through clucking like a chicken and patting a man's torso. "This demonstration of friendship was repeated several times; it was concluded by three hard slaps, which were given me on the breast and back at the same time. He then bared his bosom for me to return the compliment…"

Darwin found himself similarly under observation. He climbed a mountain with Lieutenant Sulivan, unaware that hidden natives were watching them. While Sulivan amused himself by rolling boulders down the slopes, Darwin tapped at rocks with his geological hammer; it was only later that he wondered aloud what on earth the natives would have made of their behavior.

The Fuegians shadowed Darwin's every move, copying his yawns and coughs and even his scowl when he caught them doing so. He had heard of similar abilities of mimicry among native Africans and Australians, and was respectfully impressed by it, particularly when it was a talent he found lacking among Europeans. He recalled Fuegia Basket's speedy acquisition of Portuguese when they had been quartered near Botofogo Bay, and mused that "savages" might possess a skill that civilized Europeans had allowed to atrophy.

North Atlantic

South America

MONTEVIDEO
July 26,
1832

South
Atlantic

TIERRA DEL FUEGO
Dec 18, 1832

"How can this faculty be explained? Is it a consequence of the more practised habits of perception and keener senses, common to all men in a savage state, as compared with those long civilized?"

— DARWIN'S DIARY, DECEMBER 17, 1832

It was the opportunity to compare himself with both native and assimilated Fuegians that first led him to speculate about the place of human beings, not as creatures superior to the natural world, but as extensions of it. Darwin also noted that the sheer simplicity of Fuegian life had left them with little use for cunning. If one obtained food simply by smashing a limpet off a rock, there was not much call for a hunter's sense of stealth.

The *Beagle* dwarfs a native Fuegian vessel, in a watercolor by Conrad Martens.

THE FATE OF THE FUEGIANS

In early 1833, the *Beagle* returned, to find the Reverend Matthews had already tired of his uncooperative and often hostile flock, some of whom had even plucked out his beard, hair by hair. His possessions stolen, the missionary returned to the ship, leaving the three Fuegians behind in the hope that they would "civilize" their countrymen.

By March, Darwin had noted the decline of Jemmy Button, who had reverted to Fuegian ways. "This man was poor Jemmy—now a thin haggard savage, with long disordered hair, and naked, except a bit of a blanket round his waist. We did not recognise him till he was close to us; for he was ashamed of himself, and turned his back to the ship. We had left him plump, fat, clean, and well dressed;— I never saw so complete and grievous a change."

Jemmy would eventually become a leader of the Fuegian tribes, and died in 1864, shortly after he was accused of leading a massacre of missionaries. His son, Threeboy, visited England in 1866.

The Falkland Islands

FROM TIERRA DEL FUEGO, THE *BEAGLE* SET SAIL FOR THE FALKLAND ISLANDS. THE MISSION CAME SOON AFTER THE ROYAL NAVY HAD REITERATED BRITAIN'S CLAIM TO THE ISLANDS, AND BECAUSE OF THEIR STRATEGIC IMPORTANCE, THE *BEAGLE* WOULD VISIT THEM TWICE, GIVING DARWIN THE CHANCE TO OBSERVE BOTH A NATIVE SPECIES AND A SPECIES THAT HAD BEEN TRANSPLANTED FROM EUROPE.

The *Beagle* put ashore at the Falkland Islands in 1833 and 1834. Claimed variously by French, Spanish, and English sailors, they had been named and renamed at least five times by contending powers. The latest change of fortune had seen the British retaking the islands from Argentina, a new South American state, which had proclaimed its independence from Spain just two decades earlier.

Sovereignty over the islands was disputed, and it would be several years before the Falklands would officially become a British colony. The inhabitants at the time were largely seal-hunters and whalers, and the islands retained a lawless atmosphere. Five months before Darwin's arrival, a new Argentinian governor had been murdered by his subjects; shortly after, a British warship arrived and ordered the locals to fly the Union Jack, leaving the British flag in the care of the owner of the local general store before leaving once more. British rule, however, obviously hadn't made much of an impact by the time Darwin arrived. He archly observed that of the inhabitants remaining, "half were runaway rebels and murderers."

Wild Horses

After getting used to the warmth of tropical South America, Darwin was singularly unimpressed with the Falklands, which he explored amid "boisterous and cold" weather, rain, and hail. He likened the "miserable islands" to north Wales, and noted that "except for geology, nothing could be less interesting than our day's ride."

Darwin toured parts of the island in the company of gaucho cattlemen and witnessed them bringing down a cow with bolas and lasso. They also showed him a troop of wild horses, descended from steeds left by the French in 1764. Darwin was surprised to note that the horses remained confined to the eastern end of the island, even though there was no natural barrier keeping them from spreading. He also pronounced himself "particularly curious" to discover why their early spurt in numbers had suddenly reached a plateau. One gaucho noted that the roaming stallions had a bizarre habit of forcing the mares to accompany them, which often caused them to leave their foals behind to die of starvation or exposure.

Darwin also observed an unforeseen consequence of the horses' transplantation, that they were not acclimatized to the islands' peculiar conditions: "From the softness of the ground their hooves often grow irregularly to a great length, and this causes lameness," he noted. Whereas

North Atlantic

South America

South Atlantic

FALKLAND Is.
Mar 1, 1833

*"The theatre is worthy of the scenes acted on it.
An undulating land, with a desolate and wretched aspect,
is everywhere covered by a peaty soil and wiry grass."*

— DARWIN'S DIARY, APRIL 17, 1833

Canis antarcticus

A warrah, or Falklands fox; pushed to the edge of extinction by farmers protecting their sheep.

urban horses needed to be fitted with iron "shoes" to protect them from tough European roads, out in the boggy Falklands, the ground did not provide enough wear and tear.

The Falklands Fox

Darwin was also intrigued by the warrah (the Falklands wolf or fox). A dog-like animal unique to the remote islands, the warrah were lively and inquisitive, and could be caught by a gaucho who offered meat with one hand but held a knife ready in the other.

It was in conversation with one resident, Mr. Lowe, that Darwin stumbled upon some interesting information: The common warrah was tawny-colored with a white flash on its tail, but according to Lowe, the warrah on the western island were smaller and had redder pelts. Darwin captured or purchased several specimens, and could find no immediate evidence for this claim. He hoped to pursue the nature of the warrah farther, but predicted that the concerns of newly arrived farmers were already pushing the warrah to the edge of extinction.

"Within a very few years after these islands shall have become regularly settled, in all probability this fox will be classed with the dodo, as an animal which has perished from the face of the earth."

— DARWIN'S DIARY, APRIL 17, 1833

"Some Other Planet"

AFTER DEPARTING THE FALKLANDS, THE *BEAGLE* HEADED NORTH ONCE MORE, BEFORE TURNING BACK SOUTH—REVISITING TIERRA DEL FUEGO AND THE FALKLAND ISLANDS. FINALLY, TWO YEARS AFTER LEAVING ENGLAND, ON JUNE 11, 1834 THE *BEAGLE* ROUNDED CAPE HORN AND ENTERED THE PACIFIC. ON HIS WAY UP THE WEST COAST, A NATURAL DISASTER IN CHILE CONFIRMED A THEORY THAT DARWIN HAD BEEN FORMING FOR SOME TIME. BUT IT WAS ONLY AS THE SHIP FINALLY TURNED FOR HOME THAT DARWIN STUMBLED ACROSS HIS GREATEST INSPIRATION— THE REMOTE PRISON COLONY ON THE GALÁPAGOS ISLANDS.

In late February, Darwin was dozing in a Chilean forest when the ground itself began to shake. He was in the middle of an earthquake, and for two minutes was terrified by the notion that something as solid as the ground beneath his feet could become subject to change: "There was no difficulty in standing upright; but the motion made me giddy... An earthquake like this at once destroys the oldest associations; the world, the very emblem of all that is solid, moves beneath our feet..."

In nearby settlements, stone houses collapsed, a church proved to be no less susceptible than any mundane building, and the chaos was followed by outbreaks of fire and a 20-foot (6-meter) tidal wave. Darwin speculated on the implications for days, wondering what the chances were of a similar disaster striking England. However, in the aftermath, Darwin discovered that the ground had not merely shaken, but also shifted, cracked, and risen. On a low cliff near the coast, he found a patch of dead mussels, that had clearly been underwater until only recently.

"During my walk round the island I observed that numerous fragments of rock, which form the marine productions adhering to them must recently have been lying in deep water, had been cast high up on the beach: one of these was a slab six feet by three square & about two thick. [Two by one meters, and a third of a meter thick.]"

— DARWIN'S DIARY, FEBRUARY 20, 1835

Darwin now saw how mountains might well form not in single great cataclysms, but in small increments over centuries, a little at a time, pushing seabeds above water or sinking forests beneath the sea. It was a theory that supported one already advanced in Britain by the geologist Charles Lyell, whose *Principles of Geology* Darwin had been reading.

Pacific
Ocean

South
America

MONTEVIDEO
*Apr. 26,
1833*

VALPARAISO
July 23, 1834

South
Atlantic

FALKLAND Is.
Mar. 9, 1834

ENTERED PACIFIC
June 11, 1834

The "Frying Hot Islands"

The *Beagle* set out into the open ocean, making landfall at the Chilean prison colony in the Galápagos archipelago. The volcanic islands contained conical mountains reaching above beaches of black sand, so hot that Darwin was forced to hop from foot to foot.

"We landed upon black, dismal-looking heaps of black lava," wrote FitzRoy, "forming a shore fit for pandemonium." But Darwin was ready to look beyond the islands' inhospitability to humans, and to ask if there was some other life form that might appreciate such conditions.

These islands appear paradises for the whole family of Reptiles... The black lava rocks are frequented by large, most disgusting, clumsy lizards... Somebody calls them 'imps of darkness.' — They assuredly well become the land they inhabit."

Darwin was deeply disappointed with the vegetation. After the lush greenery of the mainland, he could only find drab seaweeds and sparse plants, it was more like a desolate Arctic rock. As he went inland, he found that pathways had been smoothed through the undergrowth by heavy footfalls that reminded him of goat tracks. He rounded a corner to find a pair of giant tortoises, their shells seven feet (two meters) around, munching calmly on a cactus.

"Surrounded by the black Lava, the leafless shrubs & large Cacti, they appeared most old-fashioned antediluvian animals; or rather inhabitants of some other planet."
— DARWIN'S DIARY, SEPTEMBER 21, 1835

The Galápagos Islands

FROM CHILE THE *BEAGLE* FORGED NORTHWARD, FIRST TO PERU, THEN TO THE GALÁPAGOS ARCHIPELAGO. ALTHOUGH HE WAS INITIALLY DISAPPOINTED BY THE ISLANDS' LACK OF INSECTS, DARWIN SOON BECAME FASCINATED BY THE TINY VARIATIONS IN THE CHARACTERISTICS OF ANIMALS ON THE DIFFERENT ISLANDS— A FASCINATION THAT WOULD OCCUPY HIS THOUGHTS FOR DECADES TO COME, AND LEAD TO HIS MOST FAMOUS WORK.

The crew of the *Beagle* spent five weeks in the Galápagos Islands, while Darwin collected many specimens. The local animals, as in other remote places, were unused to predators and permitted him to get close. On one occasion, he picked up an iguana and threw it in the water, to see how it would react. It climbed out and let him pick it up again. Among the giant tortoises, Darwin was able to climb aboard one and ride it for a while, marveling at its slowness.

Food was plentiful, and Darwin dined with the crew on fresh tortoise meat, fried in its own fat. The giant tortoises of the Galápagos Islands were famous among sailors, as they made for good eating, and could be kept alive for months aboard a ship before being butchered. In the garden of Mr. Lawson, the vice-governor, Darwin found several tortoise shells in use as flowerpots, and heard from Lawson himself that the tortoises differed from island to island. This, in itself, was not news, as previous authors had observed it before. "Captain Porter," recorded Darwin, "has described those from Charles and from the nearest island to it, namely, Hood Island, as having their shells in front thick and turned up like a Spanish saddle, whilst the tortoises from James Island are rounder, blacker, and have a better taste when cooked."

But Darwin had begun to speculate on why and how such differences could occur. The thoughts that came to him about the Galápagos largely developed after he had left the islands behind, on the long sea voyage that followed, as he had time to think over the implications. In a testament to the importance (and late arrival) of this discovery in the formation of Darwin's philosophy, his "diary" account of the voyage of the *Beagle* grinds to a halt for several interpolated pages, added long after his actual time on the islands.

Darwin heard similar accounts of variation in the coloring or lengths of beak on several kinds of local birds and lizards, and commented that such "innumerable trifling details of structure" might be expected across a whole continent, but not within such a small area.

> "I never dreamed that islands, about fifty or sixty miles [80–95 km] apart, and most of them in sight of each other, formed of precisely the same rocks, placed under a quite similar climate, rising to a nearly equal height, would have been differently tenanted; but we shall soon see that this is the case."
>
> — *VOYAGE OF THE BEAGLE*

Improvised flowerpots in the governor's garden presented Darwin with a ready comparison of tortoise shells from different islands.

"But it is the circumstance, that several of the islands possess their own species of the tortoise, mocking-thrush, finches, and numerous plants, these species having the same general habits, occupying analogous situations, and obviously filling the same place in the natural economy of this archipelago, that strikes me with wonder." — VOYAGE OF THE BEAGLE

"It is the fate of most voyagers, no sooner to discover what is most interesting in any locality, than they are hurried from it; but I ought, perhaps, to be thankful that I obtained sufficient materials to establish this most remarkable fact in the distribution of organic beings."

— VOYAGE OF THE BEAGLE

Natural science in England, as Darwin already knew to his cost, was still the purview of Christian scholars. But here was a question that Darwin found compelling: if God had created all the creatures of the world, what possible reason could there be for the variations found in the Galápagos?

Already, Darwin fretted that he had missed an important area of research. He had failed to catalog his findings on an island-by-island basis, and many were already mixed together. He hoped to remedy the problem later on, by careful study of the specimens that he had already collected before FitzRoy weighed anchor and left the Galápagos Islands behind forever.

The South Pacific

ON OCTOBER 20, 1835 THE *BEAGLE* DEPARTED THE GALÁPAGOS, SETTING COURSE FOR THE DISTANT ISLAND OF TAHITI. KIND WINDS MEANT THAT THE VOYAGE LASTED JUST UNDER A MONTH, AND WHEN DARWIN ARRIVED HE FELL IN LOVE WITH THE PLACE. ALTHOUGH MUCH CHANGED FROM THE DAYS OF CAPTAIN COOK, TAHITI WAS STILL REGARDED BY MANY OF THE *BEAGLE*'S CREW AS AN ISLAND PARADISE. IT WAS ONLY WHEN DARWIN REACHED NEW ZEALAND THAT HE WAS CONFRONTED BY A STRANGE INVERSION OF THE USUAL WAY OF THINKING. COULD THE BAD "CIVILIZED" PERSON CORRUPT THE GOOD "SAVAGE"?

The South Seas had long been a matter of some discussion in the Darwin family—Charles's own grandfather, Erasmus, had once written about Tahitian marriage customs. Darwin was charmed by the island and its inhabitants, although his letters from the island remained carefully reticent about the island women's legendary semi-nudity. Darwin knew that his sisters would be reading. Instead, he kept his observations to the "finest men I have beheld," praising the menfolk's physique, tribal tattoos, and tanned skins.

A Royal Appointment

Darwin and FitzRoy entertained Queen Pomare IV (1813–77), aboard the *Beagle*. To their surprise, the 22-year-old ruler and her retinue were considerably more European in their manners than her subjects, and even seemed mildly embarrassed at the raucous songs of the sailors. Christian missionaries, observed Darwin, seemed to have enjoyed much greater success on Tahiti than the *Beagle*'s own Father Matthews had managed in Tierra del Fuego. The Tahitians sang hymns, abhorred alcohol, and praised the Lord, although Darwin noted that the women lacked a "becoming costume," and that while he liked the Queen, there was still room for improvement.

"It has been remarked that but little habit makes a darker tint of the skin more pleasing & natural to the eye of an Europæan than his own color. — To see a white man bathing along side a Tahitian, was like comparing a plant bleached by the gardeners art, to the same growing in the open fields."

— DARWIN'S DIARY, NOVEMBER 15, 1835.

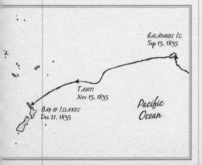

GALÁPAGOS Is.
Sep 15. 1835

TAHITI
Nov 15. 1835

BAY OF ISLANDS
Dec 21. 1835

Pacific
Ocean

"All Kinds of Vice"

Tahiti caused Darwin and FitzRoy to revisit their conclusions from Tierra del Fuego. They found the Tahitians to be kind, friendly, and welcoming. FitzRoy agreed, noting: "A more orderly, quiet, inoffensive community I have not seen in any other part of the world."

Several weeks later, after an unpleasantly rough crossing, the *Beagle* reached New Zealand, where Darwin was shocked by the contrast. Whereas Tahiti was an island of supposed savages, often better behaved than the *Beagle*'s own crew, New Zealand brought Darwin face to face with white men whose

"*The Queen is an awkquard* [sic] *large woman, without any beauty, gracefulness or dignity of manners. — She appears to have only one royal attribute, viz a perfect immoveability of expression (& that generally rather a sulky one) under all circumstances.*"

— DARWIN'S DIARY, NOVEMBER 25, 1835

The chapel at Paihia, where Darwin attended a "tedious" Christmas service.

behavior disgusted him. Although ruled by representatives of the same "superior" European culture that had produced Darwin himself, the inhabitants of the town of Kororarika could not be more different.

Darwin was baffled by the implications. How could Christian culture fail the "superior" Europeans? How could the "savage" Tahitians act in a more civilized manner? Why were some of the New Zealand Maori still heathens, while others had embraced Christianity?

On Christmas Day, Darwin attended a bilingual service at the chapel of Paihia, which he secretly pronounced "tedious" to half the congregation at any given time. He recalled in his diary that his first Christmas on the *Beagle* had been spent in Plymouth, the second at Cape Horn, the third in Patagonia, and the fourth at Tres Montes. "This fifth" was enough— he hoped to spend the sixth back in England.

"*Besides a considerable native population there are many English residents. — These latter are of the most worthless character; & amongst them are many run away convicts from New South Wales. There are many grog spirit shops, & the whole population is addicted to drunkenness & all kinds of vice... In such places the Missionaries are held in little esteem; but they complain far more of the conduct of their countrymen than of the natives. It is strange, but I here heard these worthy men say that the only protection which they need & on which they rely is from the native Chiefs against Englishmen!*"

— DARWIN'S DIARY, DECEMBER 22, 1835

Australia

ARRIVING IN SYDNEY ON
JANUARY 12, 1836, DARWIN
THE SELF-PROFESSED ENGLISH
GENTLEMAN WAS UNNERVED
BY THE SIGHT OF FORMER
CONVICTS MADE GOOD. HE
FOUND AUSTRALIA ITSELF TO
BE A CHARMING OUTPOST OF
CIVILIZATION, BUT WONDERED
IF ITS INHABITANTS WOULD
EVER SHAKE OFF THEIR LOW
ORIGINS. IN THE INTERIOR, HE
MARVELED AT NATIVE FAUNA
AND FLORA, BUT WONDERED
ALOUD IF AUSTRALIA'S UNIQUE
ECOSYSTEM COULD WITHSTAND
THE EUROPEAN INFLUX.

After months at sea, or wandering deserted islands, Sydney struck Darwin as a vast metropolis. "Ancient Rome," he wrote to his sister Susan, "in her imperial grandeur, would not have been ashamed of such an offspring."

In Australia, too, Darwin was confronted by the sight of the Old and New Worlds colliding. In 1790, Erasmus Darwin, his grandfather, had celebrated Sydney in a poem:

> Here future Newtons shall explore the skies.
> Here future Priestleys, future Wedgwoods rise.

A Wedgwood himself, Darwin was less impressed by the paucity of books, and by a city where "every other man is sure to be something between a petty rogue and bloodthirsty villain."

Convict labor had allowed Australia to leap ahead; Darwin traveled into the interior to Bathurst on new tarmac roads, and watched laborers on a sheep farm, "forty hardened, profligate men … like the slaves from Africa, yet without their just claim for compassion." He often found the Australian character unsettling, observing the outlandish attitudes that prevailed in a home where servants might be former criminals, and where children were liable to pick up bad habits and worse language from nannies of doubtful character.

"A few years since, this country abounded with wild animals; but now the emu is banished to a long distance, and the kangaroo is become scarce; to both, the English greyhound is utterly destructive. It may be long before these animals are altogether exterminated, but their doom is fixed."

— DARWIN'S DIARY, JANUARY 18, 1836

However, Darwin took great delight in the "strange character of the animals of this country." He admired parrots and cockatoos, and hoped to see some larger kangaroos. He watched duck-billed platypuses diving into a stream like water-rats, and was mildly annoyed that, when he acquired a dead one, its flexible beak had already hardened. On his hunting trip, he only managed to catch a single potoroo (rat-kangaroo), leading him to observe that the onslaught of European culture was wiping out the local fauna.

Darwin's predictions for the future of Australia rested not on its inhabitants, but on its geography and geology. He had arrived ready to believe that Australia would be a new America, but first-hand experience showed him how swiftly the coastal paradise gave way to thin pasture and forbidding desert. Coal deposits made Darwin speculate that Australia's future lay in manufacturing, not in wool and whale-oil, as "to both of these productions there is a limit."

The platypus and the potoroo. These two creatures, which are unique to Australia, fired Darwin's imagination.

He did not include the aboriginal tribesmen in his future assessment. He had met a group of them who cheerfully threw spears for him for a shilling. He was almost saddened at the friendliness of the natives, who welcomed farmers into their territory, unaware of the inevitable consequences that new technologies and a new way of life held for them.

In Hobart

The *Beagle* put in at Van Diemen's Land (Tasmania), where Darwin busied himself making geological observations. With time to reflect, Darwin even mused that he might be prepared to emigrate, not to the metropolis of Sydney, but to the more comforting world of Tasmania. "I suspect society is here on a pleasanter footing; certainly it is free from the contamination of rich convicts, and the dissensions consequent on the existence of two classes of wealthy residents."

But Darwin seemed crestfallen at the treatment of the Tasmanian aborigines, most of who had been corralled into a ghetto on an offshore island in 1833. "I fear from what I heard at Hobart Town," he wrote, "that they are very far from being contented: some even think the race will soon become extinct."

HARRIET THE TORTOISE
One Australian resident who outlived Darwin was Harriet, an ancient Galápagos tortoise believed to have been acquired by John Clements Wickham, an officer on the *Beagle*. Wickham left the navy and became a police magistrate in Australia, before retiring to France, donating his three tortoises to the Brisbane Botanic Gardens. Only correctly identified as female in the 1960s, the last survivor, Harriet (formerly Harry), died in 2006 at an estimated age of 175 years.

"The thoughtless aboriginal, blinded by these trifling advantages, is delighted at the approach of the white man, who seems predestined to inherit the country of his children."

— DARWIN'S DIARY, JANUARY 19, 1836

Homeward Bound

WITH LITTLE MORE THAN A FEW CHRONOMETRIC MEASUREMENTS TO MAKE, THE *BEAGLE*'S HOMEWARD JOURNEY WAS RELATIVELY SPEEDY, ALBEIT NOT FAST ENOUGH FOR THE HOMESICK DARWIN. "THIS ZIGZAG MANNER OF PROCEEDING IS VERY GRIEVOUS," HE WROTE TO HIS SISTER SUSAN, "IT HAS PUT THE FINISHING STROKE TO MY FEELINGS. I LOATHE, I ABHOR THE SEA AND ALL SHIPS WHICH SAIL ON IT."

The *Beagle*'s journey home took it along the underside of Australia, and then to the Keeling Islands and Mauritius in the Indian Ocean, around the Cape of Good Hope, and back to England. FitzRoy, however, insisted on one last stop in Brazil to check his chronometric calculations, while Darwin's letters fumed of his own impatience to return home.

Nevertheless, both Darwin and FitzRoy still found the time for scientific enquiry. The Keeling Islands were formed by a ring of coral around a central lagoon, but with no land nearby. Considering that the coral only flourished near the water's surface, how could it grow up from the sea bed?

Part of FitzRoy's orders included a mission to find out how far out a coral reef might begin forming. He took the *Beagle* a mile [1.6 kilometers] off shore and dropped a sounding weight in the water, but failed to hit bottom after playing out 7,000 feet [2,100 meters] of rope.

The excitement for Darwin was electric. FitzRoy's soundings made it clear that the reef stood on top of an undersea mountain. Darwin was able to piece together evidence from every part of his trip: the shifting slabs of rock in Chile; reefs close to the surface across the South Seas. He posited that the coral had formed around the top of an undersea mountain, or at the edges of an island that had sunk over time. The island, however, did not sink faster than the coral could grow, so it remained near the surface.

"Hence if we imagine such an Island, after long successive intervals to subside a few feet ... the coral would be continued upwards, rising from the foundation of the encircling reef. In time the central land would sink beneath the level of the sea & disappear, but the coral would have completed its circular wall." — DARWIN'S DIARY, APRIL 12, 1836

"Precious Nonsense"

One of the *Beagle*'s last stops was the island of St. Helena, where Napoleon Bonaparte had been exiled in 1815. Darwin stayed "within a stone's throw" of Napoleon's tomb, but affected little interest in Longwood House, the Little Corporal's last residence, which was derelict and covered in graffiti. Instead, he busied himself inspecting lava rocks, and cataloging the many plants that had taken root far from home. Some, he noticed, had traveled almost as far as him.

"Many English plants appear to flourish here better than in their native country, some also from the opposite quarter of Australia succeed remarkably well, & it is only on the highest & steep mountain crests where the native Flora is predominant." — DARWIN'S DIARY, JULY 13, 1836

The island of St. Helena, as painted by the early 19th-century English artist Robert Havell.

The derelict remains of Napoleon's house on St. Helena, close to Darwin's lodgings.

Despite his reluctance to revisit Brazil, Darwin wandered the forest there one last time, and reflected upon the wonderful opportunity he had enjoyed over the last five years. His observations in the Atlantic had led him to conclude that wondrous discoveries need not be sought in far-flung places, but could be found much closer to home if only one knew where to look. "How great would be the desire in every admirer of nature to behold, if such was possible, another planet; yet at the distance of a few degrees from his native country, it may be truly said, the glories of another world are open to him."

As the weather turned colder, and more blustery, Darwin even began to look forward to rain. He was sure that his wanderings were over, and was eager to put his voyaging behind him and return to his native land. For the rest of his life, Charles Darwin would never leave England again.

"People are pleased to talk of the ever smiling sky of the tropics: must not this be precious nonsense? Who admires a lady's face who is always smiling? England is not one of your insipid beauties; she can cry, and frown, and smile, all by turns. In short I am convinced it is a most ridiculous thing to go round the world, when by staying quietly, the world will go round with you."

— LETTER TO CAROLINE DARWIN, JULY 18, 1836

CHAPTER FOUR

OBSERVATIONS
AND
SPECULATIONS

"All England Appears Changed"

ON HIS RETURN TO ENGLAND DARWIN DISCOVERED THAT HIS LETTERS HAD ALREADY MADE HIM A MINOR CELEBRITY WITHIN THE SCHOLARLY COMMUNITY. ALTHOUGH HE STILL ENTERTAINED THOUGHTS OF BECOMING A COUNTRY PARSON, HE SOON REALIZED THAT NATURAL HISTORY SHOULD BE HIS FULL-TIME PURSUIT; ALBEIT IN A PLACE HE DID NOT CARE FOR: THE "DIRTY TOWN" OF LONDON.

The *Beagle*'s last port of call was to be on the Thames, so that FitzRoy could make one final chronometric reading by which all the others could be measured. Darwin, however, could not wait, and went ashore at Falmouth. For two evenings, he dashed through the British countryside in a succession of coaches, arriving back at The Mount late on October 4, 1836. The family was already asleep, and was hence doubly surprised to find Darwin waiting for them at breakfast.

Darwin's sister Caroline thought him awfully thin, while his father observed: "the shape of his head is quite altered." But whereas his sisters were keen to drag Darwin back into country life, and the social whirl that might find him a woman suitable to be a parson's wife, Darwin soon ran for Cambridge and London.

"But the busiest time of the whole voyage has been tranquillity itself to this last month…. I came up to town to wait for the Beagle's arrival. At last I have removed all my property from on board, and sent the specimens of Natural History to Cambridge, so that I am now a free man." — LETTER TO W.D. FOX, NOVEMBER 6, 1836

London in the 1830s was undergoing tumultuous change. After many pitch-black jungle nights, Darwin marveled at a city lit up by thousands of gaslights. Navvies carved railways through the British countryside, and the clatter of great building works filled the air through every London day.

There were casualties of such change. Government policy heeded the warnings of the late Thomas Robert Malthus, who had warned that charity could backfire, encouraging the creation of an ever-growing underclass: "The power of population is so superior to the power of the earth to produce subsistence for man, that premature death must in some shape or other visit the human race. The vices of mankind are active and able ministers of depopulation. They are the precursors in the great army of destruction, and often finish the dreadful work themselves."

London, West India Dock, 1837. Engraved by F. W. Topham after a picture by R. Garland.

London, West India Dock, 1837.

From 1837, there was a new insistence on the registration of births, marriages, and deaths, and government policy favored the gravitation of down-and-outs from the countryside toward the cities. Under the Poor Law Amendment Act of 1834, those who did not find jobs were assigned them, in workhouses. Within two years of Darwin's return, Charles Dickens would write *Oliver Twist* in protest at the conditions in which the poor lived.

Left: Thomas Malthus, who predicted dire consequences if the Earth's population continued to grow.

The Society of Dons

In Darwin's absence, Henslow had turned some of his letters into printed pamphlets, making his name already known to the academic community. He spoke at the Cambridge Philosophical Society about his discoveries of long fragments of fragile tubes of glassy material in the sand in Maldonado, in South America. Darwin thought these to be the remnants of old lightning strikes, where the energy had fused the sand into glass.

Soon afterward, he lectured at the Geological Society on the subject of the Chilean coast; his theory that the entire landmass was slowly rising up; and other speculations about the rise of atolls on sinking land in the Keeling Islands. Charles Lyell himself, whose book had been such an inspiration to Darwin, was in the audience, and told him later: "I could think of nothing for days after your lesson on coral reefs, but of the tops of submerged continents. It is all true, but do not flatter yourself that you will be believed till you are growing bald like me, with hard work and vexation at the incredulity of the world."

Lyell's warning was not unfounded. Although the Geological Society immediately welcomed Darwin as one of their own, he found that Britain's zoologists and botanists still regarded him as an amateur collector. It was not enough simply to send crate after crate of specimens back home. Unclassified and unanalyzed, they were next to useless to scholars; and Darwin discovered, to his great chagrin, that Galápagos specimens from the previous voyage of the *Beagle* six years earlier still sat, uncataloged, in crates at the British Museum.

Above: Charles Lyell, the author of *Principles of Geology*.

"I am out of patience with the Zoologists, not because they are overworked, but for their mean, quarrelsome spirit."

— LETTER TO W.D. FOX, UNDATED

Fossil Records

THROUGH HIS NEW FRIEND CHARLES LYELL, DARWIN MET THE YOUNG ZOOLOGIST RICHARD OWEN, WHO OFFERED TO COMB THROUGH DARWIN'S FINDS AT THE ROYAL COLLEGE OF SURGEONS. UNLIKE THE SNOOTIER ACADEMICS, WHO HAD SHAMED DARWIN WITH THEIR MASTERY OF LATIN SPECIES NAMES, OWEN WAS BOYISHLY ENTHUSIASTIC ABOUT DARWIN'S DISCOVERIES, PARTICULARLY THE MANY FOSSILS HE HAD SHIPPED HOME FROM SOUTH AMERICA.

Darwin's early inexperience showed: some of his fossil finds were scattered across more than one crate, and some missing pieces took weeks to uncover. But Owen was used to such a jigsaw puzzle of fossil finds, and was soon offering Darwin words of encouragement.

"Some of them are turning out great treasures," wrote Darwin to his sister Caroline. "One animal, of which I have nearly all the bones is very closely allied to the Ant Eaters, but of the extraordinary size of a small horse."

A great skull, which had taken Darwin three hours to unearth in Punta Alta, Patagonia, turned out to be even more of a find. Darwin had originally thought it to belong to a rhinoceros, but Owen pronounced it to be a giant rodent.

*Richard Owen
1804-92*

"As far as I can yet see, my best plan will be to spend several months in Cambridge, and then ... to emigrate to London, where I can complete my Geology and try to push on the Zoology."

Glyptodon

Owen's zeal was a great relief to Darwin. Owen announced that Darwin's *megatherium*, the fossil of a giant sloth, was already known to European scholars, but that Darwin's specimen helped plug previous gaps in knowledge, particularly concerning its jaw mechanism.

That, however, was far from being the only surprise. Darwin had assumed that some armor plates belonged to the *megatherium*. Owen, however, told

"Conceive a Rat or a Hare of such a size — What famous Cats they ought to have had in those days!"

— LETTER TO CAROLINE DARWIN, NOVEMBER 9, 1836

him he had discovered a creature that was previously entirely unknown; evidence of a giant armadillo that he called a *"glyptodon."* Darwin's fossils, which had sat in a crate for several years, included an extinct hippo-like creature called *toxodon*; a new ground-sloth called *scelidotherium*; and what was eventually decided to be a type of giant llama, the *macrauchenia*—which, for a while, Owen thought might have been a camel. Whether the zoological establishment liked Darwin's Latin or not, his name would be forever associated with the creatures he had unearthed in the earliest days of his voyage.

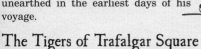

Toxodon

The Tigers of Trafalgar Square

Both Darwin and Owen agreed on what they saw as a "law of nature": that fossils of megafauna (giant prehistoric creatures) were frequently dug up on a site where smaller modern versions could be found. Darwin had dined on a small armadillo himself in Patagonia, and was intrigued by evidence of its now-extinct giant cousin. The Biblical answer, of course, was that such megafauna had fallen victim to the Great Flood, having failed to find refuge in Noah's Ark. But geologists were already asserting that evidence was lacking of any such flood in the rock record. Darwin's fossils, it appeared, had not been killed by a divine deluge.

In South America, noted Owen, there was also a "persistence of type." Where once there had been big armadillos and sloths, now there were dwarf variants of the same kinds of creatures. The two friends spent many evenings debating the evidence, such that Mrs. Owen once archly commented that when Darwin paid a visit, it would invariably lead to "tea, muscular fibre and a microscope in the drawing room."

Not long after Darwin's fossil findings were made public, workmen laying out the new London landmark of Trafalgar Square uncovered a fascinating find: the fossil remains of sabre-toothed tigers, elephants, and rhinoceroses. London's own past showed evidence of a radically different climate and inhabitants from those of the contemporary city. Darwin was sure that he would have to inhabit London himself, if he was ever to make his name as a natural scientist.

> "It is a sorrowful, but I fear too certain truth, that no place is at all equal, for aiding one in Natural History pursuits, to this odious dirty smokey town, where one can never get a glimpse, at all, that is best worth seeing in nature."
>
> — LETTER TO W.D. FOX, MARCH 12, 1837

Darwin's Finches

IT IS OFTEN THOUGHT THAT IT WAS THE TWELVE SPECIES OF FINCH THAT DARWIN FOUND ON THE GALÁPAGOS ISLANDS THAT GAVE HIM THE KEY TO THE THEORY OF EVOLUTION. HOWEVER, WHEN HE COLLECTED THE SPECIMENS, HE MISIDENTIFIED SEVERAL OF THEM AS BLACKBIRDS, GROSBEAKS, AND WRENS; AND IT WAS ONLY LATER, ONCE BACK IN ENGLAND, THAT DARWIN BEGAN TO APPRECIATE THEIR TRUE SIGNIFICANCE.

The Galápagos Islands, isolated from the South American mainland, had no native mammals until their introduction by European visitors. In contrast, the archipelago is rich in birdlife of all kinds, as well as many reptilian species, including land tortoises and, famously, land and sea iguanas. However, it was not these distant relations of the dinosaurs that caught Darwin's eye when he visited the archipelago in 1835, but its birds, in particular the mockingbirds, and a group of small, undistinguished dull brown and black birds, which, at first, he incorrectly identified.

A Case of Mistaken Identity

Once Darwin had returned to England in the fall of 1836, the work of organizing his specimens, studying them, and rewriting his journal began in earnest. He moved to his Alma Mater, the University of Cambridge, in December, where he continued to divide his studies between geology and natural history. On January 4, 1837, the day that he gave a lecture on his geological researches during the *Beagle* expedition, he also presented his mammal and bird specimens to the Zoological Society.

These bird specimens, including the mockingbirds and finches, were entrusted to John Gould, the leading British ornithologist of the day. Gould immediately recognized that the birds that Darwin had identified as finches, blackbirds, wrens, and grosbeaks, were in fact "a series of ground Finches which are so peculiar [as to form] an entirely new group, containing 12 species."

Unfortunately, Darwin had neglected to keep exact records of where he had collected each of the specimens. However, others who had also been collecting specimens, including Captain FitzRoy, had been more assiduous about recording the location of their finds.

"I THINK..."
The evidence from the finches, and other birds and mammals from the Galápagos, set Darwin on a train of thought that would culminate in the theory of evolution by natural selection. He began filling the first three of many notebooks: one for geology, one for zoology, and another for his speculations about the "transmutation" of species. In July 1836, he secretly made his first sketch of an evolutionary tree. Next to it, he wrote the simple words: "I think..."

> *"It is very remarkable that a nearly perfect gradation of structure in this one group can be traced in the form of the beak."*

What's in a Nose?

What was so special about Darwin's finches? At first sight, they seem quite unremarkable. The birds are small, between 4 and 8 inches (10–20 centimeters), and a dull brown or black in coloration. The species belong to four genera: *Geospiza*, *Camarhynchus*, *Certhidea*, and *Pinaroloxias*. Though they exhibit different behaviors and songs, what really sets them apart is the size and shape of their beaks. Once Gould had correctly identified them as finches, Darwin was able to understand the true significance of his specimens. In the 1845 edition of his *Beagle* journal, he wrote: "The most curious fact is the perfect gradation in the size of the beaks in the different species of Geospiza, from one as large as that of a hawfinch to that of a chaffinch … [t]here are no less than six species with insensibly graduated beaks… Seeing this gradation and diversity of structure in one small, intimately related group of birds, one might really fancy that from an original paucity of birds in this archipelago, one species had been taken and modified for different ends."

Galápagos Archipelago Finches

GEOSPIZA MAGNIROSTRIS

GEOSPIZA FORTIS

GEOSPIZA PARVULA

CERTHIDEA OLIVACEA

On Darwin's return to England he realized that these two "Galápagos" finches were actually unique to James Island. Other islands had other breeds.

Animal Observations

DARWIN CONTINUED TO
PRESENT PAPERS ON HIS
TRAVELS, AND WROTE ONE
OF THREE VOLUMES ON THE
BEAGLE'S JOURNEYS—THE
OTHER TWO WERE BY FITZROY
AND HIS PREDECESSOR KING.
TRUE TO DARWIN'S HOPES,
ENGLAND BEGAN TO PRESENT
HIM WITH AS FERTILE A
GROUND FOR SCIENTIFIC
ENQUIRY AS THE FAR-FLUNG
CORNERS OF THE WORLD.

Darwin continued to mull over the wide variance in human beings that he had witnessed on the voyage of the *Beagle*. It was widely assumed that European, Christian culture represented a superior form of humanity; but Darwin realized that he was no better adapted to life in the wilderness of Tierra del Fuego than Jemmy Button had been to a dinner party.

The Fuegians, thought Darwin, were undoubtedly men, but were arguably closer to animals than to "civilized" man.

The Greatest Fortune

On March 28, 1838 Darwin went to the zoological gardens on an unusually warm day. It was, he wrote, "the greatest piece of fortune," as the sun was sufficient to lure many otherwise listless animals from their cages. He observed a rhinoceros kicking and rearing, and unnerving a nearby elephant, which ran off, "squeeling & braying like half a dozen broken trumpets."

But Darwin was most fascinated by Jenny, the latest in a series of orang-utans acquired by the Zoological Gardens, but the first to survive long enough to be exhibited. Clad in a dress, Jenny had recently been presented to the Duchess of Cambridge. Now she was paraded before onlookers "in great perfection," by a keeper who offered her an apple but refused to hand it over. While Darwin watched, "she threw herself on her back, kicked & cried, precisely like a naughty child. She then looked very sulky & after two or three fits of pashion, the keeper said, 'Jenny if you will stop bawling & be a good girl, I will give you the apple.'"

The ape's display of what appeared to be human emotion was impressive enough, but what really struck Darwin was the idea that Jenny had genuinely understood what her keeper was saying. In his private notebook, he wrote furiously: "Let man visit Ourang-outang in domestication, hear expressive whine, see its intelligence when spoken [to], as if it understood every word said —see its affection to those it knows, —see its passion & rage, sulkiness & very extreme of despair."

"She certainly understood every word of this, &, though like a child, she had great work to stop whining, she at last succeeded, & then got the apple, with which she jumped into an arm chair & began eating it, with the most contented countenance imaginable."

— LETTER TO SUSAN DARWIN, APRIL 1, 1838

Darwin was not the first to notice the human-like behavior of the orang-utan. The creature's name is Malay for "person of the forest."

Questions on Selection

Darwin's thoughts turned to other creatures, and how their characteristics might be steered through the generations. The fact that the best dogs, pigeons, or horses might be bred to maintain those traits was a fundamental part of country life. In fact, thought Darwin, while such breeders were selecting the best traits, farmers already recognized that such selection could occur through natural means. In a pamphlet by the aging bird breeder Sir John Sebright, Darwin found the best support yet for his growing hypothesis.

Darwin had started to suspect that different pigeon breeds were descended from a common ancestor.

"A severe winter," wrote Sebright, "or a scarcity of food, by destroying the weak and the unhealthy, has had all the good effects of the most skilful selection. In cold and barren countries no animal can live to the age of maturity, but those who have strong constitutions; the weak and the unhealthy do not live to propagate their infirmities."

Before long, Darwin had begun to compile a form letter, "Questions About the Breeding of Animals," which he circulated among farmers in 1839. It posed 21 innocuous queries about animal traits: how they endured without help; whether newly bred traits faded with times; and on the fertility of crossbreeds.

"All information is valuable," Darwin wrote, "regarding any crosses whatever, between different wild animals, either free or in confinement, or between them and the domesticated kinds." But it was his 19th question that contained his underlying obsession: "Can you give the history of the production in any country of any new but now permanent variety, in quadrupeds or birds, which was not simply intermediate between two established kinds?"

Darwin was asking the breeders the ultimate question: Had any of them seen a new species come into being, one that was created not by God, but by simple selection?

"Man in his arrogance thinks himself a great work, worthy the interposition of a deity. More humble and I believe true to consider him created from animals."

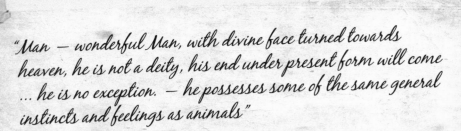

"Man — wonderful Man, with divine face turned towards heaven, he is not a deity, his end under present form will come ... he is no exception. — he possesses some of the same general instincts and feelings as animals"

— **Darwin's Notebooks**

"Better Than a Dog"

NOW APPROACHING THE
AGE OF 30, DARWIN BEGAN
TO CONSIDER MARRIAGE,
APPROACHING IT WITH THE
SAME DISPASSIONATE HUMOR
AS HE CATALOGED BEETLES.
THE LUCKY MRS. DARWIN
WOULD BE HIS COUSIN, EMMA
WEDGWOOD, IN A MATCH THAT
WOULD MAKE DARWIN'S OWN
UNCLE JOS HIS NEW FATHER-
IN-LAW. MUCH AS PIGEONS
OR DOGS MIGHT BE BRED
FOR THEIR BEST TRAITS, THE
UNION ENSURED THAT THE
FAMILY FORTUNE REMAINED
INTACT.

Darwin had begun to think about marriage, regarding a wife as "that most interesting specimen in the whole series of vertebrate animals, Providence only knows whether I shall ever capture one or be able to feed her if caught." Only half in jest, he took a scrap of blue paper and listed the pros and cons of finding himself a bride.

On paper, the prognosis did not look good. Darwin weighed a "nice soft wife on a sofa" against all the things he would never be able to do: learn French; visit Europe; travel to the United States; go up in a balloon; or go off, alone, to Wales. "Poor slave," he wrote to himself, "you will be no better than a Negro." And yet, he countered, it would not be possible to remain a bachelor forever, "friendless and cold and childless." Inadvertently, he quoted his explosive argument with FitzRoy on the *Beagle*: "There is many a happy slave."

Darwin had found his answer. Now he only needed to ask the question.

"DAY OF DAYS"
Although Darwin referred to it as the "Day of Days," the Sunday when he popped the question was something of an anti-climax. His proposal took Emma so much by surprise that she went off to teach Sunday School as usual. It was only Uncle Jos who wept "tears of joy" when the couple went to seek his permission. As for Charles and Emma, the future Mrs. Darwin wrote "I believe we both looked very dismal."

MARRY

Children — (if it Please God)

Constant companion, (& friend in old age) who will feel interested in one,

Object to be beloved & played with.

Better than a dog anyhow

Home, & someone to take care of house

Charms of music & female chit-chat.

These things good for one's health.

~~Forced to visit & receive relations~~

but terrible loss of time.

Mrs. Darwin

Emma Wedgwood (1808–96) was the youngest of Uncle Jos's seven children, and had practically grown up with Darwin, who still remembered her as a messy child. She had visited Europe, where she studied the piano in Paris under Chopin, and briefly lived near Geneva with an aunt. Darwin himself had accompanied her home from Paris in 1827. However, Emma was also a devout Christian, and Darwin struggled to conceal his religious doubts.

As his notebooks reveal, Darwin's thoughts were largely on his own interests and comfort, particularly that which Emma's dowry would bring. Against his father's advice, he blurted at least some of this to Emma, who laughed it off, noting that: "he is the most open, transparent man I ever saw, and every word expresses his real thoughts."

The couple were married in Maer on January 28, 1839, a Wedgwood parson presiding. The young couple rushed for the train, and spent their wedding night in London, although the date in Darwin's notebooks shows that he also found the time to jot down some thoughts about turnips.

Emma Darwin, painted by George Richmond in 1840.

Not Marry

No children, (no second life), no one to care for one in old age.

What is the use of working in without sympathy from near & dear friends—who are near & dear friends to the old, except relatives

Freedom to go where one liked

choice of Society & little of it.

Conversation of clever men at clubs

Not forced to visit relatives, & to bend in every trifle.

to have the expense & anxiety of children

perhaps quarelling

Loss of time.

cannot read in the Evenings

fatness & idleness

Anxiety & responsibility

less money for books &c

if many children forced to gain one's bread.

(But then it is very bad for ones health to work too much)

Perhaps my wife wont like London; then the sentence is banishment & degradation into indolent, idle fool.

"Marry — Marry — Marry Q.E.D."

A Quiet War

LONDON LIFE BECAME PROGRESSIVELY MORE UNBEARABLE FOR THE DARWINS, WITH CHARTIST RIOTS IN THE STREETS, AND DARWIN HIMSELF STRUCK DOWN BY A MYSTERY ILLNESS. THE BIRTHS OF HIS FIRST TWO CHILDREN PROVIDED EVEN MORE REASON TO FLEE TO THE COUNTRYSIDE. AND HIS WRITING BEGAN TO REFLECT HIS THOUGHTS ON HIS OWN FRAILTIES, AND THOSE OF HIS INFANT SON.

The drafting of a People's Charter in 1837 led to a series of protests around Britain by "Chartists"—people demanding fair elections and electoral districts, and voting rights for all men over 21, not merely the rich. The Chartists did not merely demand reform among the voters, but also among the elite politicians who represented them: calling for the abolition of the property qualification for Members of Parliament, and for the institution of salaries. Chartism was an attack on members of the property-owning classes, people like Darwin, who could conceivably have used his father's money to forge a career in politics, much as he had done with the sciences. Mrs. Darwin, meanwhile, thought the sentiments of the pamphleteer Thomas Carlyle "full of compassion and good feeling but utterly unreasonable. Charles keeps on reading and abusing him."

Although Darwin was supposed to be writing about coral reefs, the violence on the streets caused him to speculate more about its counterpart in the natural world. Darwin had already noted that gardeners talked of the sudden and accidental growth of hardier, stronger seedlings. In such cases, the stronger varieties would undoubtedly prevail unless weeded out for unexpected side-effects—hardier beans, perhaps, might not taste so good. But what of the weaker varieties? For every tiny

"It is difficult to believe in the dreadful but quiet war of organic beings going on in the peaceful woods and smiling fields."

— **DARWIN'S NOTEBOOK ON TRANSMUTATION, 1838–9**

The Chartist thinker Thomas Carlyle (1795–1881) studied as a preacher but lost his faith, turning instead to politics and social criticism.

Metropolitan policemen (in top hats) break up a Chartist demonstration in London.

"When two races of men meet, they act precisely like two species of animals, — they fight, eat each other, bring diseases to each other &c, but then comes the most deadly struggle, namely which have the best fitted organization, or instincts (i.e. intellect in man) to gain the day."

— DARWIN'S NOTEBOOK ON TRANSMUTATION, 1838–9

change for the better, there might be hundreds of changes for the worse, fated to die without reproducing. Darwin saw the world as a "vigorous battle between strong & weak," not only for plants, but for animals in the wild, and even the men fighting in the streets.

Survival of the Fittest

Nor did he see himself as one of the strong. He had suffered from fevers and occasional heart palpitations throughout the voyage of the *Beagle*, although nobody had taken them seriously—Captain FitzRoy, instead, had scoffed at Darwin as "a martyr to seasickness." Now back on land for good, Darwin had discovered that stress and overwork would cause him to suffer powerful headaches and violent stomach upsets that could leave him bedridden for days. His ailments would continue for the rest of his life, and caused him to wonder if he, too, was destined to be one of the losers in the struggle for survival.

Darwin's eldest son, William Erasmus Darwin, was born in December 1839, and soon became a new source of scientific enquiry. Armed with information about Jenny the orang-utan's response to a mirror, Darwin showed one to his son to compare reactions. He also recorded "Mr. Hoddy Doddy's" first manifestations of certain emotions, from smiles to frowns, in a relentlessly scientific manner, in a journal that he kept for the next 17 years about the development of all his children.

Although Darwin's notebooks described William as an experimental subject: "touching sole of foot with spill of paper, (when exactly one week old), it jerked it away very suddenly & curled its toes, like person tickled," his letters showed him to be a proud and anxious father, particularly when his own father noted William's sickly nature.

"Dear old Doddy, one could write for ever about him. I am grieved to hear my father, who is kindness itself to him, thinks he looks a very delicate child." William was put on a special diet, and Darwin began to fret about consanguinity: had the Darwin–Wedgwood pedigree bred disadvantaged, weaker offspring?

"Aged just thirty-three, with my eldest son William Erasmus. This was also the year in which I published my book on coral reefs"

1842

"During first week, yawned, streatched [sic] himself just like old person – chiefly upper extremities – hiccupped – sneezes sucked, Surface of warm hand placed to face, seemed immediately to give wish of sucking, either instinctive or associated knowledge of warm smooth surface of bosom. – cried & squalled, but no tears."

CHAPTER FIVE

DARWIN
AT
DOWN

Down House

DARWIN MOVED TO DOWNE, THEN A SMALL VILLAGE TO THE SOUTHEAST OF LONDON, TO ESCAPE THE PRESSURES OF CITY LIFE. IT WAS THERE THAT HE RAISED HIS FAMILY, COMPLETED HIS WORK *ON THE ORIGIN OF SPECIES* AND HIS OTHER BOOKS, AND LATER DIED. DOWN HOUSE IS NOW IN THE CARE OF ENGLISH HERITAGE, WHICH HAS OPENED IT TO THE PUBLIC AS A MUSEUM AND PERPETUAL MEMORIAL TO DARWIN AND HIS WORK.

In 1842, in response to the civil unrest that was affecting London at the time, Darwin decided to move his family to the village of Downe. Although it has since been subsumed within the London suburb of Bromley, Kent, at the time when Darwin moved there Downe was a quiet village some 14 miles (23 kilometers) to the southeast of central London.

Home Improvements

Down House (confusingly with no "e," unlike the village of Downe) was originally built in 1650 for a well-to-do farmer, and was extended in the late 18th century. Darwin purchased the house for the sum of £2,200 from the local rector, the Rev. Drummond. Ever the scientist, Darwin noted that: "I was pleased with the diversified appearance of the vegetation proper to a chalk district."

Over the years, the Darwins made their own home improvements and additions to the house and grounds. In 1843, Darwin opened a large bay window in the front of the house to take advantage of the views of the surrounding countryside. In 1849, he had a tree-lined avenue laid out in the grounds, which he named the Sandwalk, where he took his daily constitutional and which he used as his "thinking path." In 1858, the family added a new drawing room and extended the main entrance to the house. Further alterations continued into the 1870s, providing the family with a new dining room, smoking room, billiard room, verandah, and a study.

The Darwins at Down

When Darwin moved to the country, his family consisted of just his wife Emma, his son Erasmus, and his daughter Anne. Emma, however, was pregnant again, but tragically their infant daughter Mary Eleanor died in October, 1842, just a month before the move. A year later, Henrietta (b. 1843) was the first of the growing Darwin family to be born at Down, and she was followed by George (b. 1845), Elizabeth (b. 1847), Francis (b. 1848), Leonard (b. 1850), Horace (b. 1851), and Charles Waring Darwin (b. 1856).

DOWNE

Villagers in Down added an "e" to its name in order to avoid association with County Down in Ireland.

"I feel sure that I shall become deeply attached to Down, with a few improvements — it will be very difficult not to be extravagant there."

Down House still
stands today, and
is a lively museum
to the life and work
of Darwin.

*"After several fruitless searches in Surrey and elsewhere,
we found this house and purchased it … Few persons can
have lived a more retired life than we have done."*

From School to Museum

Charles Darwin died on April 19, 1882, aged 73; and Emma
survived him by 14 years, dying in 1896. In 1907, Down House
was sold to a Miss Olive Willis, who established a girl's boarding school there. One of the school's residential halls was named
after its former owner. The school moved to new premises in
1922. In 1927, the surgeon Sir George Buckston Browne bought
the house and presented it to the British Association for the
Advancement of Science, together with an endowment to
ensure its preservation as a museum and memorial to Darwin.
The house opened as a museum on June 7, 1929.

Unfortunately, Buckston Browne's endowment could not
meet the running costs of the museum, and in 1953 the property was donated to the Royal College of Surgeons of England.
In 1962, Sir Hedley Atkins, later President of the Royal College
of Surgeons, moved into the house together with his wife to
assume the role of honorary curator. In 1996, Down House was
bought by English Heritage with a grant from the Wellcome
Trust. It was restored with funds raised by the Natural History
Museum and with a grant from the Heritage Lottery Fund, and
reopened to the public in April 1998.

HOME-MAKING

**Darwin began planting
flowers in the garden,
to remind Emma of her
home at Maer Hall, and
to take her mind off her
father's terminal illness.
He placed sticks in the
grounds to mark his
planned tree-planting.
His brother Erasmus
was less than impressed,
and called the place
"Down-in-the-mouth."**

Revolutions

EVEN AS DARWIN RETREATED FROM LONDON, LOSING HIMSELF IN HIS RESEARCH AND IN THE LIFE OF A COUNTRY GENTLEMAN, THE WORLD WAS UNDERGOING A PERIOD OF RADICAL CHANGE. SOME OF THESE DEVELOPMENTS WOULD SHAPE DARWIN'S THINKING ON THE STRUGGLE BETWEEN SPECIES, WHILE OTHERS CHANGED THE SPEED WITH WHICH IDEAS COULD BE COMMUNICATED.

"During the first part of our residence we went a little into society, and received a few friends here," wrote Darwin, "but my health almost always suffered from the excitement, violent shivering and vomiting attacks being thus brought on." Down soon became a permanent retreat, and but for occasional family visits and outings to the library, Darwin rarely left his new home, even as the world around him underwent a great and often violent period of change.

In Washington, D.C. in 1844, the results of a Baltimore election were transmitted at record speed through Samuel Morse's electric telegraph. In Britain, Darwin was now able to send letters with a prepaid "apostille"—a postage stamp affixed to the envelope. Technology was racing ahead like a species of its own. Some inventions, like the mournful musical instrument patented by Adolphe Sax in 1846, had unknown potential. Others, like the use of general anesthesia by Crawford Long, would transform the medical world.

A Specter Haunting Europe

In 1848, Karl Marx and Friedrich Engels published *Manifest der Kommunistischen Partei*—the *Manifesto of the Communist Party*. It was aimed squarely at upsetting the old order, of which Darwin was a part. According to the *Manifesto*, the same working-class radicals who were agitating for the vote in the cities were destined to wrest control of society itself from the current ruling class. Targets of the *Manifesto*'s rhetoric included the owners of the means of production, distribution, and exchange; in other words, establishment figures such as the Wedgwoods, whose factories created wealth for them, only a fraction of which was distributed to the workers.

Darwin never recorded his opinions on the Communists; in fact, he only used the word "communism" in an anthropological sense, when discussing early marriage customs. But Darwin believed very strongly in the rules of propriety, and in the need to keep one's underlings at arm's length. Mrs. Darwin, meanwhile, had trouble with the family servants, and once even dismissed a cook for being "too cute."

Even as the Darwins came to terms with their position as masters of their house, Marx and Engels were writing of an eternal battle between different forces within humankind: "The history of all hitherto existing societies is the history of class struggles. Freeman and slave, patrician and plebeian, lord and serf, guild-master and journeyman, in a word, oppressor and oppressed, stood in constant opposition to one another, carried on an uninterrupted, now hidden, now open fight, a fight that

Karl Marx and Friedrich Engels were the founding fathers of Communism.

Karl Marx

Friedrich Engels

Left: The March Revolution called for the unification of the many German states into one empire, and risked igniting conflict over a "Greater Germany."

each time ended, either in a revolutionary reconstitution of society at large, or in the common ruin of the contending classes."

In 1848, Europe was rocked by a series of revolutions, including uprisings in France, Germany, Hungary, and Spain. Elsewhere in the world, there were also changes afoot. Ireland was wracked by a great famine, causing many deaths, but also huge emigration to the United States. In the United States, a conference debated whether the Declaration of Independence should apply equally to women; not even the Chartists had previously demanded that women should be allowed to vote. As Chartist demonstrations turned to riots in the city, Darwin sat in his country study, and wrote of barnacles and coal seams.

The Great Chartist "Monster" Rally on Kennington Common in London, which threatened to turn into a revolution in Britain.

Darwin Orphaned

The year 1848 also saw the death of Darwin's father after a long illness. "He attempted to speak about you this morning," wrote Caroline Darwin to her brother, "but was so excessively overcome he was utterly unable; we begged him not to speak as we knew what he would have said; the least emotion or excitement exhausts him so, it is quite dangerous." Darwin's own children were too young to understand their father's grief, and Henrietta ("Etty"), only five years old, wept "bitterly out of sympathy," although for what, she did not know.

Darwin found comfort in Emma's sympathy, but not in her reliance on the promised afterlife. It only served to remind Darwin of something his father had told him some years earlier: that religious doubts were best hidden from a devout spouse.

"Before I was engaged to be married, my father advised me to conceal carefully my doubts, for he said that he had known extreme misery thus caused with married persons."

The Thinking Path

DARWIN'S REGIME AT DOWN INCORPORATED A SERIES OF TREATMENTS INTENDED TO ALLEVIATE HIS ILLNESS. OVER THE YEARS, HE INCORPORATED MEDICAL NECESSITY INTO HIS WORKING DAY, INTERSPERSING HIS CORRESPONDENCE AND RESEARCH WITH PRACTICAL EXPERIMENTS IN DIFFERENT CORNERS OF THE ESTATE.

The Sandwalk was not originally part of the grounds at Down House, but was rented from Darwin's neighbor John Lubbock. Darwin eventually bought it outright.

Darwin moved the entire family to Malvern in 1849 to be near him while he took a series of "water treatments" at a spa run by Dr. James Gully. The remedies that Gully offered included an early start to the day, cold footbaths, showers, and long walks, wearing a damp cloth close to the skin. Darwin stayed for 16 weeks, and found that, no matter how unpleasant, the ordeal lessened his unknown illness.

Back at Down, he developed a rigid daily routine that incorporated elements of Dr. Gully's torments. He would rise early (at 5 am in summer) and exercise, at first on the roads near the house. At noon, he would march out to the Sandwalk at the far end of the grounds, and take five circuits of the path through the trees. Then, whatever the weather, he would take a shower beneath a specially built water tower that his children likened to a church steeple.

His daughter Henrietta remembered that "in early days we used generally to take his midday walk with him, for I remember after Malvern our standing outside his douche hearing the rush of water & his groans from the shock & cold, & stamping of feet & then when he was up & dressed we were allowed to pull the string & see the remains of the water come down. He then used to set off at a run & we with him."

More often, however, Darwin was alone. He would arrive in the drawing room at the same time each day to read his letters, and again at a later hour to read the newspaper. Sometimes, especially in winter to save on heating, he would eat dinner with his children by the fire in their schoolroom. Darwin's food, however, was relentlessly bland and unspiced at his doctor's orders. Otherwise, Darwin pottered in his study. Dr. Gully recommended only two hours of hard thinking per day, leaving Darwin to devote mornings to his science, and afternoons to the easier matter of his correspondence. His chair was fitted with trundle wheels so he could move from shelf to desk without getting up, while his study was scattered with specimens, both from his travels and from his own greenhouses. In one corner of the room, a curtain discreetly concealed a commode; although Darwin's illness rarely left him completely, he refused to let stomach upsets or retching interfere with his work.

"The diversity of the breeds is something astonishing. Compare the English carrier and the short-faced tumbler, and see the wonderful difference in their beaks, entailing corresponding differences in their skulls."

— ON THE ORIGIN OF SPECIES

Darwin was fascinated by the diversity of pigeons, which seemed to him to be a domestic analog of natural variation among the Galápagos finches.

The Pigeon Fancier

Darwin's walks became an inevitable part of his working day, sneaking beyond the prescribed two hours in his study, into long solitary exercises in thought. His children soon learned not to disturb him as he ambled along his "Thinking Path," while his detours to the greenhouses or flowerbeds formed part of his work in progress.

In the 1850s, Darwin became fascinated with pigeons, joining two London clubs, and keeping up to 90 birds in an aviary on the Down House grounds. Since all were descended from a single "wild" variety, he was intrigued by the variations that had been introduced by breeders, and noted that this single, "aboriginal" ancestor was the father of perhaps 20 new breeds. "Altogether at least a score of pigeons might be chosen, which if shown to an ornithologist, and he were told that they were wild birds, would certainly, I think, be ranked by him as well-defined species."

Seeds and Leaves

Darwin's experiments even extended to the vegetable patch, where, among other things, he kept watch on 28 varieties of cabbage. The seeds, he noticed, were almost identical, and he found it hard to tell cabbage seeds from those of broccoli or cauliflower, despite the great difference in the appearance of the adult plants.

"The explanation is obvious," he wrote. Farmers did not care about the look, feel, or taste of cabbage seeds, as, unlike cereals, the seeds were not what people ate. Instead, "many useful variations in their leaves and stems have been noticed and preserved from an extremely remote period, for cabbages were cultivated by the old Celts."

"I have kept every breed which I could purchase or obtain, and have been most kindly favoured with skins from several quarters of the world."

— ON THE ORIGIN OF SPECIES

Illimitable Wonders

DARWIN DEVOTED EIGHT YEARS TO THE STUDY OF MARINE INVERTEBRATES, INCLUDING BARNACLES, RELIVING HIS GLORY DAYS ABOARD THE *BEAGLE* AND BECOMING AN EXPERT IN A TINY CORNER OF THE ZOOLOGICAL WORLD. EVEN AS HE WORKED IN AN ACCEPTABLE FIELD, HE SECRETLY PREPARED HIS THEORY OF "TRANSMUTATION OF SPECIES," BUT FEARED THE REACTION IT MIGHT CAUSE. INSTEAD, HE LOOKED ON AS AN ANONYMOUS AUTHOR PUBLISHED A SIMILAR IDEA, WHICH WAS RECEIVED WITH WIDESPREAD HORROR.

By 1846, Darwin had reached the end of his *Beagle* specimens, but found new inspiration in the very last one: a crustacean parasite that he found in the final bottle of samples, stuck to the shell of another creature. The "illformed little monster," he realized, was a previously undiscovered form of barnacle, for which the adult male was a tiny twin-penised creature almost invisible to the naked eye. "But here comes the odd fact," enthused Darwin, "the male, or sometimes two males ... become parasitic in the sack of the female, & thus fixed & half-embedded in the flesh of their wives they pass their whole lives & can never move again."

"I do not know of any other case where a femal invariably has two husbands.... Truly the schemes & wonders of nature are illimitable."

— LETTER TO CHARLES LYELL, JUNE, 1849

Darwin's researches into the new find, which he nicknamed "Mr. Arthrobalanus," used the growing power and portability of microscopes, allowing him to investigate creatures previously undiscovered. As Darwin's interest in barnacles widened, he enlisted the aid of travelers all over the world, including Arctic explorers. He even tracked down Syms Covington, his former servant from the *Beagle*, now a farmer in Australia, asking him to fish new examples from the sea. Covington obliged the following year with a packet of useful finds, wrapped in local newspapers that, to Darwin's delight, included mentions of other *Beagle* shipmates. He subsequently published the exhaustive books *Living Cirripedia* and *Fossil Cirripedia*, becoming the pre-eminent authority on barnacles through the ages.

Vestiges of Creation

However, Darwin's barnacle work may have been a deliberate distraction to keep him from his secret project. He had already completed much of his preliminary work on what was to become his famous *On the Origin of Species*, but feared the controversy that would ensue if he published it. Instead, he wrote a strange living will to Emma, asking her to set aside £400 from his estate after his death, and to use it to publish his work.

Soon after Darwin had set down his "most solemn & last request," he was able to witness the likely outcome of his posthumous intentions. An anonymous author published *The Vestiges of the Natural History of Creation* (1844), controversially

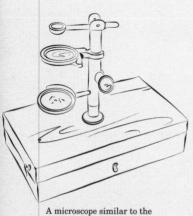

A microscope similar to the one that Darwin used to study his specimens on the *Beagle*'s voyage.

"I have just finished my sketch of my species theory. If, as I believe, my theory in time be accepted even by one competent judge, it will be a considerable step in science." — LETTER TO EMMA DARWIN, JULY 5, 1844.

suggesting that God was not a careful architect of the universe, but an absent law-maker who had left worlds to form and life to "transmutate" into new species by the action of random forces. The *Vestiges* shocked the establishment, both through the implication that humans might have similarly sprung from lower animals, and in the suspicion that the author only mentioned God at all as a sop to the public, and that his arguments comprised veiled atheism.

The author of the *Vestiges* was only revealed as the essayist Robert Chambers in the book's 12th edition of 1884, some 13 years after Chambers himself had died. Although Darwin noted that the author's "geology strikes me as bad, & his zoology far worse," he would engage in indirect debate with the then anonymous Chambers for decades to come, through reviews and revisions to both *Vestiges* and Darwin's own books.

Darwin's all-encompassing examination of barnacles, both living and extinct, made him the world expert on the subject.

"RED IN TOOTH AND CLAW"
Alfred Tennyson's poem "In Memoriam A.H.H." (1849) was the product of 17 years' work, a meditation on grief but also an examination of many modern issues troubling Victorians, including atheism and the growing debate over "transmutation" fostered by the publication of the *Vestiges*. It summarized, poetically, Darwin's developing thought on the natural world as a place of fierce struggle.

"Who trusted God was love indeed
And love Creation's final law
Tho' Nature, red in tooth and claw
With ravine, shriek'd against his creed."

"Our Bitter and Cruel Loss"

In 1851, Darwin was inconsolable at the death of his "favourite child," his nine-year-old daughter Annie. He believed, perhaps rightly, that she had inherited his own stomach condition, and was forced to watch her swift decline from violent bouts of vomiting and diarrhea. Emma Darwin sought consolation in her faith, but her husband found himself unable to believe in an afterlife, and, over time, in any God that could be recognized from Christian scripture.

Darwin began to worry that his mysterious condition, whatever it might be, could be passed on to his descendants. His eldest daughter, Annie, began to suffer from fevers and stomach upsets, although by March 1851, the ailments seemed to have passed. "She inherits, I fear" wrote Darwin, "my wretched digestion."

When Annie's symptoms returned later in the month, Darwin resolved to take her to see Dr. Gully. With Henrietta for company, they left the heavily pregnant Emma behind at Down House, and traveled to the Malvern Hills.

Darwin had initially left Annie there to convalesce, but was soon called back from Down House as her condition worsened. With Dr. Gully unable to offer any help, Annie succumbed to symptoms redolent of typhoid, commencing with a "bilious fever," before passing into a coma from which she never woke up. Darwin himself suffered a relapse after witnessing some of her final convulsions.

Doubtless through the grieving Emma, there was some talk among the family that the "angelic" Annie was a real angel now, causing her younger sister, Henrietta, to fret that she was not good enough, in fact, would never be good enough to enter Heaven herself. Darwin, for his part, eschewed the temptation to decorate Annie's grave with pious Victorian statuary, and opted instead for a blunt, unadorned headstone that proclaimed her to be: "A dear and good child."

"She was my favourite child; her cordiality, openness, buoyant joyousness and strong affections made her most loveable."

"We have lost the joy of our household and the solace of our old age."

Annie's Box
The Darwins gathered up Annie's meager possessions and locked them out of sight. It was not until the turn of the 21st century that Charles Darwin's great-great grandson, Randal Keynes, discovered Annie Darwin's writing case inside a family heirloom chest. The box included some of her calligraphy, her pens and ink, samples of embroidery, a ribbon, a lock of her hair, and, as a final mournful addition, a map to her grave in Malvern.

"When I am dead, know that many times, I have kissed & cryed over this."

The End of Faith

It is widely believed that Annie's death signaled an abrupt end to Charles Darwin's Christian faith. In fact, he had been drifting away from Christianity for many years, and had been skeptical ever since he first understood that non-believers like his father were doomed, in Christian eyes, to eternal torture for their sincerely held agnosticism.

"The disbelief crept over me at a very slow rate," Darwin wrote, "but was at last complete."

During his *Beagle* days, he had been sure enough of the Bible to quote it at his shipmates to settle arguments, but in the years since, he had slowly come to question many of its pronouncements. Years spent studying the natural sciences, particularly geology and zoology, left him with little time for the Old Testament, which he regarded as "no more to be trusted than the sacred beliefs of the Hindoos, or the belief of any barbarian." Nor did Darwin the scientist have much time for the miracles of the New Testament, and their explanation as "metaphors or allegories" was no help if they were supposed to be the foundation of faith.

Faith alone, wrote Darwin, was not proof. "Hindoos, Mahomadans and others might argue in the same manner and with equal force in favour of the existence of one God, or many Gods, or as with the Buddists [*sic*] of no God." By 1849, he had stopped attending church with his family, and would go for walks instead. In 1850, he reveled in Francis Newman's new book *Phases of Faith*, which discounted the historical veracity of much of the Bible and repudiated the notion of Hell.

Annie Darwin was her father's favorite, and he mourned her loss for the rest of his life.

Annie's grave was rather plain by the standards of the Victorian gentry; a sign of Darwin's lack of faith in the afterlife.

"What a book a devil's chaplain might write on the clumsy, wasteful, blundering, low, and horribly cruel works of nature!"

— LETTER TO JOSEPH HOOKER, JULY 13, 1856

The Great Exhibition

THE YEAR OF ANNIE'S DEATH WAS ALSO THE YEAR OF AN INTERNATIONAL FAIR IN LONDON'S HYDE PARK. THE GREAT EXHIBITION AND ITS FAMOUS VENUE, THE CRYSTAL PALACE, WERE A HIGH POINT OF THE VICTORIAN AGE, WITH EXHIBITS FROM AS FAR AFIELD AS CHINA AND AUSTRALIA. HOWEVER, AMONG THE ENGINES, VEHICLES, AND ARTWORKS, THE THING THAT LEFT THE MOST LASTING IMPRESSION ON DARWIN WAS THE WOOL OF A NEW BREED OF SHEEP.

The Great Exhibition of 1851 was the first of the World's Fairs, an international convocation of the newest technologies and oldest traditions, held in the middle of 1851 in a vast, purpose-built glass building, the "Crystal Palace" in Hyde Park, so large that it was built around pre-existing trees. The Crystal Palace was a soaring Victorian success, attracting six million visitors (almost a third of the United Kingdom's population at the time), and making a profit so hefty that the surplus was used to set up three museums and a scholarship fund.

With even Queen Victoria reportedly enthusing about her visit to the Exhibition as the "greatest day of my life," Darwin was not one to pass up such an opportunity. He took the entire family with him and stayed with Erasmus at his town house, a short cab ride away from Hyde Park, for the whole week. Darwin returned to the Great Exhibition again and again, although his children soon grew bored with it and were left in their uncle's care.

The Exhibition prompted memories of Darwin's days aboard the *Beagle*. Van Diemen's Land had sent a sad little display of its dwindling aboriginal population, accompanied by predictions, matching Darwin's own, of the natives' looming extinction. The display from New South Wales included an aboriginal dictionary assembled by white settlers, but no examples of aboriginal culture.

Despite Darwin's excitement, the trip had its cost; his medical condition flared up once more, and it took another week for him to recover.

The Crystal Palace, planned and built in Hyde Park in just nine months, was itself one of the most enduring wonders of the Great Exhibition. Moved to a new location after the event, it was destroyed by fire in 1936.

A Famous Visitor Reports

"It is a wonderful place – vast, strange, new and impossible to describe. Its grandeur does not consist in one thing, but in the unique assemblage of all things. Whatever human industry has created you find there, from the great compartments filled with railway engines and boilers, with mill machinery in full work, with splendid carriages of all kinds, with harness of every description, to the glass-covered and velvet-spread stands loaded with the most gorgeous work of the goldsmith and silversmith, and the carefully guarded caskets full of real diamonds and pearls worth hundreds of thousands of pounds. It may be called a bazaar or a fair, but it is such a bazaar or fair as Eastern genii might have created. It seems as if only magic could have gathered this mass of wealth from all the ends of the earth – as if none but supernatural hands could have arranged it thus, with such a blaze and contrast of colours and marvellous power of effect. The

multitude filling the great aisles seems ruled and subdued by some invisible influence. Amongst the thirty thousand souls that peopled it the day I was there not one loud noise was to be heard, not one irregular movement seen; the living tide rolls on quietly, with a deep hum like the sea heard from the distance."

— **Charlotte Brontë,**
Letter to P. Brontë, 1851

The Mauchamp-Merino

Darwin was not merely in search of distraction or diversion. He visited the Zoological Gardens—as a member, he was permitted to attend after hours—and chatted with several associates who were serving as judges of the many exhibits. In particular, he was intrigued by reports of wool from a farm in Mauchamp, France. After the birth in 1828 of a merino ram with remarkably "long, smooth, straight, and silky wool," its owner, one Farmer Graux, had used the unique newcomer to breed an entire flock by 1833.

"So peculiar and valuable is the wool," wrote Darwin, "that it sells at 25 per cent. above the best merino wool: even the fleeces of half-bred animals are valuable, and are known in France as the 'Mauchamp-merino.'"

Darwin found the speed of development interesting enough, but noted that although shepherds were only interested in the wool, the new variety of sheep exhibited other deviations from the norm: "the first ram and his immediate offspring were of small size, with large heads, long necks, narrow chests, and long flanks; but these blemishes were removed by judicious crosses and selection."

"If the Mauchamp and Ancon breeds had originated a century or two ago, we should have had no record of their birth."

CHAPTER SIX

ON THE ORIGIN OF SPECIES

A Matter of Honor

IN 1858, DARWIN WAS SHOCKED TO RECEIVE A DRAFT OF A PAPER "ON THE TENDENCY OF VARIETIES TO DEPART INDEFINITELY FROM THE ORIGINAL TYPE" FROM ALFRED WALLACE, A YOUNG NATURALIST IN BORNEO. DARWIN APPEALED TO THE "JUDGEMENT AND HONOUR" OF CHARLES LYELL, ASKING IF IT WOULD BE A CRIME TO PUBLISH HIS OWN THEORIES FIRST, EVEN THOUGH HE ONLY KNEW OF WALLACE'S INTENTIONS AND IDEAS THROUGH PRIVATE CORRESPONDENCE. EVENTUALLY, DARWIN AND HIS ASSOCIATES ARRANGED A GENTLEMANLY COMPROMISE: THE PAPERS WERE TO BE READ OUT ON THE SAME DAY.

Alfred Russel Wallace (1823–1913) was a young naturalist whose main area of enquiry was initially the Amazon rainforest. Inspired by Darwin's *Beagle* voyage, and other expeditions like it, Wallace spent four years in Brazil, chronicling the flora, fauna, and inhabitants of the region, and amassing many specimens. However, almost his entire haul sank with the ship that was supposed to bring him back to England in 1852. Rescued after ten days in an open boat, Wallace was able to salvage just a few papers and two books' worth of writings from memory, but lost his chance to make an entire career on the back of his findings.

Refusing to admit defeat, Wallace left England again in 1854 and spent eight years in the Malaysian archipelago, where he identified a thousand new species of beetles and a gliding tree frog, and began extensive work on "biogeography": the classification of the Earth into distinct zones of interrelated or dependent species.

Wallace speculated that: "Every species has come into existence coincident both in space and time with a closely allied species." This idea, later known as the Sarawak Law, led to further thoughts, summarized in his 1855 paper "On the Law Which has Regulated the Introduction of Species." In it, Wallace noted that if it were possible to steer the development of domestic animals in such wildly different directions by selective breeding, then surely such variations were just as possible in the natural world. But, wrote Wallace, whereas domestic animals maintained a tendency to keep to their original pedigree, "there is a general principle in nature which will cause many varieties to survive the parent species, and to give rise to successive variations departing further and further from the original type."

Wallace observed: "The life of wild animals is a struggle for existence," and began to speculate even further about the biological mechanism that led to the creation of new species. In search of support and advice on publishing a new paper, "On the Tendency of Varieties to depart indefinitely from the Original Type," he sent a draft version from Borneo to a British scholar he admired: Charles Darwin.

"All my originality, whatever it may amount to, will be smashed."

Pacific Ocean

BORNEO

Australia

Indian Ocean

"This MS. work was never intended for publication, and therefore was not written with care."

Forestalled!

Darwin was horrified. Charles Lyell had warned him in the past that someone was sure to pre-empt him if he did not publish his theories. "Your words have come true with a vengeance," he wrote to Lyell, "that I should be forestalled."

There was no more waiting for posthumous infamy, as he had planned. "But," fretted Darwin to Lyell, "as I had not intended to publish any sketch, can I do so honourably, because Wallace has sent me an outline of his doctrine?" After much soul-searching, Darwin guiltily decided to present a paper of his own to the Linnean Society of London. Admitting that he had never planned to present his theory of natural selection until facing the threat of a rival, Darwin decided to read his paper at a joint presentation, so that both he and Wallace would publish their views on the same day. On July 1, 1858, with Wallace still in the Far East, his paper was read out to the Linnean Society alongside a hastily concocted extract from Darwin's unpublished manuscript, called "The Perpetuation of Varieties and Species by Natural Means of Selection." Darwin did not attend either. He was at home, grief-stricken at the death from scarlet fever of his infant son Charles Waring Darwin.

Darwin's section included a forceful footnote—part apology, part boast—pleading that he had never planned on publishing his work, but that it was "sketched in 1839, and copied in 1844, when the copy was read by Dr. Hooker, and its contents afterwards communicated to Sir Charles Lyell." Thereby, he protested for all to see that he had thought of the theory long before, and even cited witnesses to support his claim. Had he not done so, this book might have been called *Wallace's Notebook*, and Darwin confined to its footnotes as a man who knew a lot about barnacles.

Alfred Russel Wallace

Alfred Russel Wallace, whose new theory was coincidentally similar to the one Darwin had been keeping to himself for years.

The Linnean Society crest and motto, *Naturae Discere Mores*: "To Learn the Ways of Nature."

The Abominable Volume

DARWIN PUBLISHED THE FIRST EDITION OF *ON THE ORIGIN OF SPECIES BY MEANS OF NATURAL SELECTION, OR THE PRESERVATION OF FAVOURED RACES IN THE STRUGGLE FOR LIFE* ON NOVEMBER 24, 1859. THE BOOK WAS AN INSTANT HIT WITH BOTH SCIENTISTS AND LAY READERS, AND THE FIRST EDITION OF 1,250 COPIES QUICKLY SOLD OUT. DURING HIS LIFETIME, DARWIN PUBLISHED A FURTHER SIX REVISED EDITIONS.

Considering the revolutionary content of the Darwin and Wallace papers, they caused very little stir in the scientific community at the time, although Darwin's allusions to a pre-existing manuscript functioned as excellent bait to publishers. Later that month, Darwin signed a contract with the publisher John Murray for a full-length work on the topic. His agent for the transaction was Charles Lyell, who managed to get Murray to agree to publish the book sight unseen.

Darwin was unsure if Murray would even publish it. As far as Darwin was concerned, any modern geology textbook ran "slap counter to Genesis," and his thoughts on animals and plants were of a similar nature. Regardless, he asked Lyell if he needed to undertake some pre-emptive damage control.

"Would you advise me to tell Murray that my book is not more un-orthodox than the subject makes inevitable. That I do not discuss the origins of man. That I do not bring in any discussion about Genesis, &c. &c., and only give facts, and such conclusions from them as seem to me fair."

Although Darwin had claimed to have a complete manuscript, preparing his work for publication involved thorough revisions, rewrites and considerations of what he called his "rag of a hypothesis." The work in progress was sent to Lyell and their friend Joseph Dalton Hooker for their approval and comments. Lyell was troubled by the implications for the origin of mankind, whereas Hooker shamefacedly reported that his wife had accidentally put part of the manuscript in a drawer, from which his children had taken almost a quarter of the entire book to use as drawing paper.

A little over a year later, the book had been printed and was ready to go on sale. Regarding it as a rather dull discussion of scientific matters, John Murray had to be talked out of printing a mere 500 copies.

ON

THE ORIGIN OF SPECIES

BY MEANS OF NATURAL SELECTION,

OR THE

PRESERVATION OF FAVOURED RACES IN THE STRUGGLE FOR LIFE.

By CHARLES DARWIN, M.A.,

FELLOW OF THE ROYAL, GEOLOGICAL, LINNEAN, ETC., SOCIETIES;
AUTHOR OF 'JOURNAL OF RESEARCHES DURING H. M. S. BEAGLE'S VOYAGE
ROUND THE WORLD.'

LONDON:
JOHN MURRAY, ALBEMARLE STREET.
1859.

The right of Translation is reserved.

STYLE AND CONTENT
One of the great strengths of *On the Origin of Species* is its readable style, which made it accessible to scientists and lay readers alike. The 1859 edition consists of an introduction and 14 chapters. In the introduction, Darwin revisits the *Beagle* expedition of 1831–6, referring to the animals that had first given him the idea for the theory of evolution by natural selection. He then moves chapter by chapter, outlining the theoretical basis and evidence for the evolution of species.

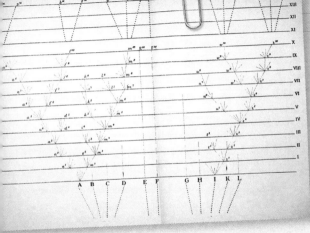

"So much for my abominable volume, which has cost me so much labour that I almost hate it."

Sold Out

On the Origin of Species was published on November 24, 1859, at a price of 15 shillings. Darwin ensured that a copy was sent out to the gracious Alfred Russel Wallace in Borneo. "God knows," wrote Darwin to Wallace, "what the public will think."

Amazingly, the first edition of 1,250 books sold out two days before the official publication date. A second edition of 3,000 copies was quickly printed and issued on January 7, 1860. In all, six editions of *Origin* were published during Darwin's lifetime, and each time he revised the text to deal with any counter-arguments that had been raised by its critics. The third edition came out in 1861 with a number of additions and an introductory appendix entitled, "An Historical Sketch of the Recent Progress of Opinion on the Origin of Species." The fifth edition, published on February 10, 1869, incorporated more changes.

Darwin heard that a group of Lancashire laborers had pooled their money to buy a copy, so he asked Murray to make the next edition more affordable. The ensuing sixth edition used smaller print and sold at half the price of the previous edition, and went on sale on February 19, 1872, with a new chapter designed to silence recent critics. The word "On" was dropped from the title and Darwin employed the word "evolution" for the first time.

"In the survival of favoured individuals and races, during the constantly recurring struggle for existence, we see a powerful and ever acting form of selection."

A photograph of Darwin around the time of the publication of *On the Origin of Species.*

Variation

THE FIRST PART OF *ON THE ORIGIN OF SPECIES* DREW ON THE JOINT PRESENTATION OF DARWIN'S AND WALLACE'S WORK. IT BEGAN BY ARGUING THAT THE VERY DEFINITION OF A "SPECIES" WAS OPEN TO QUESTION, AS EVEN ANIMALS OF THE SAME SPECIES USUALLY DISPLAYED WIDELY DIFFERING ATTRIBUTES. ONE OF ITS MOST POWERFUL IDEAS, FROM A CHRISTIAN POINT OF VIEW, WAS THAT CREATION WAS NOT YET FINISHED AND THAT NEW SPECIES CONTINUED TO DEVELOP.

Despite his claim to Lyell that he would not include humankind in his analysis of the natural world, Darwin dragged in human examples in his very first chapter.

"Everyone," wrote Darwin, "must have heard of cases of albinism, prickly skin, hairy bodies &c., appearing in several members of the same family. If strange and rare deviations of structure are truly inherited, less strange and commoner deviations may be freely admitted to be inheritable."

However, the bulk of Darwin's argument rested on animals. He observed that human beings had been steering the development of domestic animals, such as dogs, since the Stone Age. It was presumed that dogs had once been wolf-like animals that somehow fell into the company of early humans, and that every modern variety of dog was produced "by the crossing of a few aboriginal species."

Darwin noted that while the greyhound, the bloodhound, the bulldog, and the spaniel were all different, they were nevertheless all still dogs. The use of "artificial selection" in their breeding methods might create diverse breeds, but it did not create an entirely new species.

In fact, Darwin noted that signs of an original ancestor would sometimes pop up in their descendants. From his own experiences with pigeons, he recalled that the blue coloring of the rock pigeon (*Columba livia*) would often reassert itself in widespread varieties of other birds.

"I can feel no doubt that all our domestic breeds have descended from the Columba livia with its geographical sub-species."

Columba livia, the original breed of bird from which all pigeons could claim descent.

Incipient Species

Darwin went on to argue that the scientific community only assumed that it had properly classified the species it discussed. Science's understanding of the world was only as good as its access to information. Darwin himself had discovered dozens of new animals and plants on his *Beagle* voyage. Who was to say that there were not intermediate varieties, as yet undiscovered? If animals X and Z were thought to be separate species, the discovery of a "missing link" (a term he got from Charles Lyell), a previously unknown "Animal Y" related to the other two, would force the scientific community to reclassify all three, X, Y, and Z, as part of the same species.

For this reason, Darwin argued that variations between the animals of a given species were not beneath the notice of

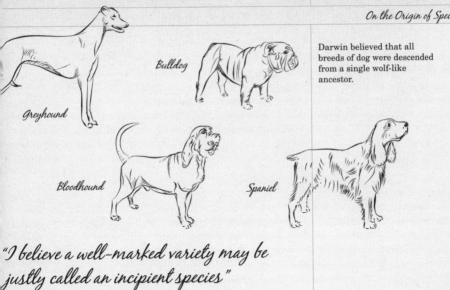

Greyhound

Bulldog

Bloodhound

Spaniel

Darwin believed that all breeds of dog were descended from a single wolf-like ancestor.

"I believe a well-marked variety may be justly called an incipient species"

scientists. In fact, given enough time and the benefits of hindsight, such variations might be seen as the first stirrings of a separate and new species, manifesting at first in trivial differences that could reinforce each other, flourish under new and unexpected conditions, or spread through the first mutant's descendants. Conversely, uncountable numbers of such "incipient species" might have been killed off before they had the chance to develop, particularly if their new traits were to their biological disadvantage.

This simple assertion carried explosive potential for the religious establishment. It suggested, however obliquely, that Creation was not the single, completed construction exercise reported in the Book of Genesis. Would Noah have needed 90 varieties of pigeon aboard the Ark, or could he have simply taken a pair of *Columba livia*, and left it to later breeders to create the later varieties themselves?

LAMARCKISM

Darwin's thoughts in *On the Origin of Species* drew on the work of his own grandfather, Erasmus, whose *Zoonomia* posited that "all warm-blooded animals have ... the power of acquiring new parts." This led to the assumption that if, say, a creature had to stretch its neck to reach high branches on a tree, it could pass on its elongated neck to its descendants, eventually creating a neck like that of the giraffe. This idea was popularized by the French biologist Jean Baptiste Lamarck (1744–1829).

Our modern understanding of natural selection instead posits that giraffe-like creatures with longer necks were more likely to reach the food in higher branches, and hence more likely to survive in lean times. Over many generations, the shorter-necked creatures would die out, and the longer-necked offspring would flourish. The process could repeat and reinforce its effects countless times.

Natural Selection

DARWIN'S CENTRAL THESIS WAS THAT RANDOM EVENTS— CHANGES IN CLIMATE OR AVAILABILITY OF FOOD, LANDSCAPE OR THE PRESENCE OF PREDATORS—WERE JUST SOME OF THE MANY UNCOUNTABLE FACTORS THAT LED A SPECIES TO ADAPT TO ITS SURROUNDINGS. HE CALLED THIS CONCEPT "NATURAL SELECTION," AS A COUNTERPOINT TO THE "ARTIFICIAL SELECTION" THAT COULD BE IMPOSED BY ANY BREEDER OR GARDENER WORKING WITH DOMESTIC VARIETIES.

Given that living things are involved in a constant struggle for existence, *On the Origin of Species* suggested that "any variation, however slight and from whatever cause proceeding, if it be in any degree profitable to an individual of any species, in its infinitely complex relations to other organic beings and to external nature, will tend to the preservation of that individual, and will generally be inherited by its offspring."

Darwin's years of study furnished him with dozens of examples. An insect with a longer proboscis was more likely to gain more nectar from certain plants. Fortune favored the slimmer, faster wolf. Natural selection, for Darwin, was not merely a matter of being better, faster, or stronger. It could be used to explain other variations in the animal kingdom that otherwise made no sense.

There was also, Darwin suggested, a case for "sexual selection," in which an animal's choice of a mate was determined by personal criteria. The ostentatious, glittering plumage of the peacock attracted the attention of the peahen. Over many generations, brighter-colored peacocks with bulkier tails had attracted more mates and passed on their characteristics to more descendants. Meanwhile, less colorful peacocks had failed to mate and their drabber characteristics had died with them.

"I have called this principle, by which each slight variation, if useful, is preserved, by the term of Natural Selection, in order to mark its relation to man's power of selection."

If nectar were found deep inside a flower, Darwin predicted that some insect would evolve a long enough proboscis to reach it.

Divergence of Character

Darwin had realized that one creature's success might spell disaster for other animals in its neighborhood. He raised the idea of a "carnivorous quadruped" (a predator such as a fox or lion) and noted that if its numbers reached a certain tipping point, it would be forced to seek "new kinds of prey, either dead or alive; some inhabiting new stations, climbing trees, frequenting water, and some perhaps becoming less carnivorous." Darwin's hypothetical predator would have to adapt or die. If it kept to its old hunting grounds, it might eat all the prey, and in doing so cause its own species to starve to death. But in seeking new sources of food or ways of living, the species would be forced to diversify.

"The expression often used by Mr. Herbert Spencer, of the Survival of the Fittest, is more accurate, and is sometimes equally convenient."

THE SURVIVAL OF THE FITTEST

After reading *On the Origin of Species*, the economist Herbert Spencer drew on its ideas in his 1864 book, *Principles of Biology*. "This survival of the fittest," he wrote, "which I have here sought to express in mechanical terms, is that which Mr. Darwin has called 'natural selection', or the preservation of favoured races in the struggle for life." Darwin liked Spencer's term so much that he incorporated it into the fifth and sixth editions of his own book. However, modern evolutionary biologists prefer to use the term "natural selection," as the definition of "fitness" requires an impossible judgement of what conditions might favor particular attributes. Furthermore, "survival of the fittest" is arguably a tautology: survival implies fitness already.

Herbert Spencer (1820–1903), who first suggested that the "survival of the fittest" could apply to society itself.

An original ancestor might have been adapted to roaming on flat plains. Its descendants, as they spread, might need to acclimatize to rocky mountains in one region; climb trees in another; or scavenge carrion instead of hunting fresh meat. Over many generations, Darwin argued that new environments might cause his hypothetical quadruped to form varieties so divergent that its distant descendants could be regarded as separate species.

There was, thought Darwin, "no limit to the amount of change, to the beauty and infinite complexity of the coadaptations between all organic beings, one with another and with their physical conditions of life, which may be effected in the long course of time by nature's power of selection."

Darwin's theory helped explain seemingly bizarre characteristics, such as the peacock's tail, although Wallace had his doubts.

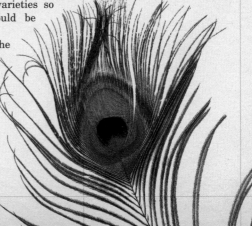

Natura non Facit Saltum

Sure that he would face criticism from many quarters, Darwin devoted part of *On the Origin of Species* to a discussion of problems within his theory. With Biblical Creation discounted in his mind, Darwin appealed to the fossil record to fill in some of the gaps from the prehistoric past, uniting the disciplines of biology and geology. Pre-empting any challenge to put his theory to the test, he examined the fiendishly complicated human eye.

Darwin realized that his theory of natural selection would require much further study and support. He attempted to predict some of the most obvious areas of enquiry, both to outline possible areas for research, and to pre-empt critics who might have otherwise accused him of fudging certain issues.

Transitional Varieties

One problem Darwin saw in his theory was the absence or, at least, rarity of transitional varieties. If species did diverge through tiny changes over long periods of time, then surely there would be ample evidence in the natural world of intermediate stages in such development?

Instead, Darwin suggested that intermediate varieties were more likely to become swiftly extinct, as they were supplanted by their better-adapted descendants.

"By my theory these allied species have descended from a common parent; and during the process of modification, each has become adapted to the conditions of life of its own region, and has supplanted and exterminated its original parent and all the transitional varieties between its past and present states."

Darwin had first pondered this problem some 20 years earlier. Notebook jottings, made shortly after his return from the *Beagle* voyage, drew on his observations of coral reefs, which were only alive very close to the surface, and for which earlier generations were as dead as stone. The tree of life, he once wrote in a notebook, "should perhaps be called the coral of life, base of branches dead; so that passages cannot be seen." Similarly, in his chapter on transitional varieties, he noted that

Some woodpeckers evolve colorful plumage, while others evolve camouflage.

"The crust of the earth is a vast museum."

> *"If it could be demonstrated that any complex organ existed, which could not possibly have been formed by numerous, successive, slight modifications, my theory would absolutely break down. But I can find out no such case."*

examples might be hidden from sight. The natural world, perhaps, was the wrong place to look for them; instead, the place to search for birds with less fully formed wings, apes with less developed hands, or slower species of tiger would be within the fossil record.

Inimitable Perfection

Darwin also recognized that a certain leap of faith was required to believe that a creature such as a bat could have evolved from an ancestor without wings. It was easy for Darwin to believe that an increase in muscle-power might give a tiger more reach, and hence increase its ability to catch food. But even he recognized that more complex attributes—flight, for example, or extremely complicated organs—would take truly epic lengths of time to evolve.

"Can we believe that natural selection could produce, on the one hand, organs of trifling importance, such as the tail of a giraffe, which serves as a fly-flapper, and, on the other hand, organs of such wonderful structure, as the eye, of which we hardly as yet fully understand the inimitable perfection?"

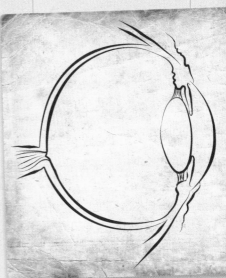

Darwin believed that even the human eye, complex as it is, could be explained through natural selection.

However, Darwin appears to have been teasing his future critics. *Natura non facit saltum*, he wrote in Latin, "Nature does not make a jump." Seizing upon the eye as an example, he noted how the most simple of beginnings—a nerve sensitive to light—could be seen as one end of a long chain of developments in optic senses, corneas, rods, and cones, ultimately reaching a recognizable mammalian eye.

If even something as complex as the eye was explicable, argued Darwin, then surely lesser organs were more so. In particular, organs might become adapted from one purpose to another; Darwin posited that human lungs may have begun life as aquatic swim-bladders.

However, Darwin also called on theorists to consider multiple possible causes. One might assume, he pointed out, that a green woodpecker was green for the purpose of camouflage, whereas the presence of other colors of woodpecker led him instead to believe that green woodpeckers were steered in that evolutionary direction by sexual selection, rather than an inherited characteristic that helped them hide from predators.

The Geological Record

**DARWIN BOTH APPEALED TO
THE GEOLOGICAL RECORD
TO SUPPORT HIS HYPOTHESIS,
AND DISCUSSED ITS "IMPER-
FECTIONS" AS ONE OF THE
PROBLEMS WITH HIS THEORY.
HE NOTED THAT APPARENT
SUDDEN CHANGES IN DOMINANT
SPECIES SUGGESTED THAT
ONCE A SPECIES HAD DEVEL-
OPED STRONG ENOUGH
ADVANTAGES THROUGH
NATURAL SELECTION, IT COULD
SOON SUPPLANT MANY FORMER
COMPETITORS.**

Sure that the religious establishment would question his assertion of there having been enough time for species to diverge, Darwin returned to the matter of geology. Beginning with something that he was sure his critics could agree on, he noted that anyone could walk along the British coastline and see for themselves the awful slowness of coastal erosion.

"A man must for years ... watch the sea at work grinding down old rocks and making fresh sediment, before he can hope to comprehend anything of the lapse of time, the monuments of which we see around us." And yet, argues Darwin, all can agree that the action of the sea on the coastline does eventually achieve an alteration of that coastline. Even if the tide only wears at the rocks "for a short time twice a day," it is clear that the sea does eat into cliffs or deposit new sediment over time.

Drawing on the findings of geologists, including his friend Charles Lyell, Darwin observed that it was possible to add together differing levels of sedimentary rock strata. With the Paleozoic strata at 57,154 cumulative feet (17,420 meters), Secondary strata at 13,190 feet (4,020 meters), and Tertiary strata at 2,240 feet (682 meters) it was possible to find, in England alone, 72,584 feet (22,123 meters) of fossil record of ancient sedimentary deposits. Having already reminded his readers of the slowness of the action of the tides, Darwin challenged them to speculate on how long it would take for ancient tides to deposit layers of sediment that amounted to such an immense build-up of sand.

"What time this must have consumed!"

Darwin added that the Mississippi River was assumed to deposit sediment at the rate of perhaps 600 feet (180 meters) in a hundred thousand years. He regarded this, if anything, as a conservative estimate, and yet it still presented compelling evidence that the world had endured not for thousands of years, nor even millions, but for billions.

Parallelism

Darwin anticipated that some would criticize him for taking no notice of parallelism, whereby identical animals would apparently arise in distant localities. He argued that although, for example, birds might

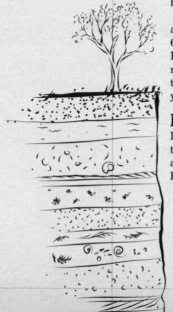

Contrary to the widely held belief that the world was only a few thousand years old, Darwin pointed to rock strata as evidence that it was much older.

"The inhabitants of each successive period in the world's history have beaten their predecessors in the race for life"

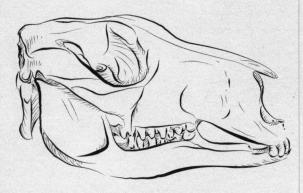

Darwin's theory was supported by a fossil record that unveiled seemingly anomalous finds; for example, the skulls of marsupials that had once flourished in prehistoric Europe.

appear to have leapt into being all over the world at exactly the same time, such an apparently "immediate" change might require only a relatively short period of geological time. Birds would only need to evolve once in one part of the world, for their offspring to spread far and wide in a relatively small number of generations.

Similarly, the geological record encouraged natural scientists to remember that the world was in a state of permanent change. Merely because certain fish might be found in widely distant lakes, it did not necessarily mean that the lakes had not once been parts of a much larger, prehistoric body of water. As a case in point, Darwin noted that the inland Aral and Caspian Seas both appeared to contain shellfish that were related in some form to shellfish in distant Madeira. Perhaps the Aral and Caspian Seas has once been part of a vast super-ocean?

In fact, far from disproving Darwin's theory, the geological record might be used to support it. Fossils showed, for example, that marsupials had once flourished in Europe. Although wiped out by unknown conditions in the Northern Hemisphere, this class of mammals had endured in Australia.

Darwin made no attempt to discuss specific causes. He offered no theory on what cataclysm might have befallen, for example, the dinosaurs. Instead, he merely noted that something had changed the conditions under which the dinosaurs had formerly flourished. In a relatively short space of time, the fossil record of large reptiles was replaced by a surge in the numbers of smaller mammals. In straightforward terms of the "survival of the fittest," the local requirements for such fitness had swiftly, radically altered, and with them, the odds that once favored the formerly dominant species had turned against them.

The fossil record suggested that the Aral and Caspian Seas were once part of a much larger ocean.

Geographical Distribution

IN THE MANY YEARS THAT DARWIN HAD KEPT HIS THEORY TO HIMSELF, HE HAD HAD AMPLE OPPORTUNITY TO TEST SOME OF HIS HYPOTHESES. INSTEAD OF SIMPLY THEORIZING ON CERTAIN ELEMENTS, HE HAD BEEN ABLE TO CONDUCT HIS OWN EXPERIMENTS AND INCORPORATE THE DATA OF SEVERAL SMALL BUT SIGNIFICANT DISCOVERIES. IT WAS ONLY ON CERTAIN MUCH LARGER CONCEPTS THAT HE APPEALED TO THE RESEARCHES OF HIS PEERS.

Darwin allowed that many migrations might occur through "accidental means," such as seeds being washed ashore on new islands. He was, however, most surprised to discover that no botanists had investigated the hardiness of seeds when transported across the ocean, and resolved to conduct his own experiments.

Soaking 87 different varieties of seed in saltwater for 28 days, Darwin discovered that 64 of them survived the ordeal, and could be planted and grown into mature plants. A smaller number survived immersion for six months.

Darwin conducted further tests with plants, branches, stems, and fruits, in an effort to determine their buoyancy, and the length of the period they might reasonably be expected to float on the open sea. He relished his discovery that some seeds, such as hazel nuts or asparagus, did not float in their ripe form but became remarkably seaworthy when dried, and would still germinate afterwards.

He concluded that some 14 per cent of his test varieties might reasonably be expected to float on the sea for a month, while maintaining their powers of germination on arrival on a new shore.

Using data gleaned from other researchers who built on his pioneering experiments, Darwin speculated that such plants on a hypothetical island would be able to germinate on another island up to 900 miles (1,450 kilometers) away, if washed into the sea and floated to their new home by a flood or some other accidental agency.

Other accidental means considered by Darwin included birds, who might eat seeds and excrete them elsewhere. Experiments in the London Zoological Gardens had already concluded that seeds could still be grown after they had been eaten and regurgitated by an owl.

"In the course of two months, I picked up in my garden 12 kinds of seeds, out of the excrement of small birds."

Means of Dispersal

Darwin was intrigued by the possibilities presented by climate change, not only for forcing new adaptations to species' circumstances, but also for hiding prehistoric pathways used by migrating species. "[A] region, when its climate was different may have been a high road for migration, but now be impassable." Creatures might walk across ice, or, if marine in origin, travel to new places during floods.

For discussion of this possibility, Darwin grudgingly referred (see below) to the theories of Edward Forbes, who had suggested that land bridges might have once connected islands that were now cut off from one another. Hence, perhaps, during an ice age when sea levels were lower, animals might have found new places to live, or new conditions under which they were forced to develop new adaptations. This theory was old news by 1859, and could even be seen in speculations by Charles Lyell in the 1830s that suggested, only half in jest, that geology offered new evidence for the possibility of Atlantis, or at least something like it, once linking Africa to South America.

However, Darwin had his doubts about some of Forbes's conclusions, since he implied that "scarcely a single island exists which had not been recently united to some continent." The concept of continental drift, and the modern theory of plate tectonics, would not become established in scientific thought until long after Darwin's death.

The naturalist Edward Forbes (1815–54) suggested that islands might once have been connected by land bridges that were subsequently submerged.

> *"I have never, of course, alluded in print to my having independently worked out this view."*

Late in life, Darwin would comment that he had "lost nothing" and "gained much" by delaying the publication of his theory of natural selection for the two decades that elapsed since he conceived it around 1839. His one regret was that the delay allowed Edward Forbes to beat him into print with a theory about the influence of the Ice Age on the migration of species. In his private autobiographical notes, Darwin admitted it was vain, but pleaded there was probably proof somewhere that he had written to Hooker about his idea before Forbes—a similar appeal to that mounted against Wallace. The "of course" was a gesture of grudging respect; Forbes died in 1854, in his thirties, and Darwin appears to have regarded a claim on his scientific legacy to have been ungentlemanly.

> *"Change of climate must have had a powerful influence on migration."*

CHAPTER SEVEN

ACCLAIM
AND
CRITICISM

"Damnable Heresies"

THE REACTION TO THE PUBLICATION OF *ON THE ORIGIN OF SPECIES* WAS MIXED. ATHEIST OR AGNOSTIC SCIENTISTS WERE LARGELY ELATED BY ITS BOLD SUGGESTIONS. HOWEVER, THE RELIGIOUS ESTABLISHMENT WAS LEFT AGHAST; ALTHOUGH, UNLIKE DARWIN, SOME CHRISTIANS STILL THOUGHT IT POSSIBLE FOR HIS THEORY TO BE COMBINED WITH AN ALLEGORICAL INTERPRETATION OF GOD AS THE DESIGNER OF THE EVOLUTIONARY PROCESS.

Despite Darwin's efforts to avoid discussing the implications of his theory for the origins of humankind, many reviewers were quick to read between the lines. One of the first, in the *Athenaeum*, scoffed that Darwin was an acolyte of the anonymous author of the *Vestiges of the Natural History of Creation*, and that his unspoken conclusion was one of "men from monkeys." However, while the critical reaction was heated, it was nowhere near as angry as Darwin had previously feared; the *Vestiges* had, at the very least, prepared the minds of the public to a certain extent. In fact, Darwin and his publishers were surprised at how widely the book was read. It became a runaway success outside the scientific community, as members of the public bought copies in order to examine the controversial claims for themselves.

Darwin could also count on his friends and associates, most of whom offered enthusiastic support. He had buttered up many acquaintances with a diligent campaign of letter-writing, and some advanced copies that were judiciously sent to opinion-formers. There was some success through "accidental means," as when the London *Times* commissioned an anonymous review from Darwin's good friend Thomas Huxley, who heaped praise upon it. Darwin pronounced Huxley a "good & admirable agent for the promulgation of damnable heresies."

Thomas Huxley
1825-95

A Bitter Satire

Karl Marx, the co-author of the *Manifesto of the Communist Party*, was glad to see a view of the world that discounted any notion of a divine Creator, and relished the suggestion that the natural world was in a constant battle for survival. "Darwin's book is very important," he wrote to Engels, "and serves me as a basis in natural science for the class struggle in history." They would later begin work on *Dialectics of Nature*, which seized upon *On the Origin of Species* in support of their own approach to history: "Darwin did not know what a bitter satire he wrote on mankind, and especially on his countrymen, when he showed that free competition, the struggle for existence, which the economists celebrate as the highest historical achievement, is the normal state of the animal kingdom."

Others liked the book for radically different reasons. The author Charles Kingsley wrote an enthusiastic letter to

Karl Marx
1818-83

"Our ancestor was an animal which breathed water, had a swim bladder, a great swimming tail, an imperfect skull, and undoubtedly was an hermaphrodite! Here is a pleasant genealogy for mankind."

Darwin, entirely untroubled by Darwin's implicit dismissal of much of the Bible. "I have gradually learned to see," wrote Kingsley, "that it is just as noble a conception of Deity, to believe that He created primal forms capable of self development into all forms needful." Darwin would add this comment to later editions, hoping to use it to lessen the ire of the religious establishment.

Charles Kingsley
1819-75

However, it was impossible to please everyone. For some, there was already too much pro-religious sentiment in the book. Harriet Martineau, Erasmus Darwin's old flame, loved the book but thought it "a pity" that Darwin had referred to God at all, as it left the possibility that a divine being had started the entire process in motion. "I rather regret," she wrote, "that C.D. went out of his way two or three times … to speak of 'the Creator' in the popular sense of the First Cause."

There was a sharper critical reaction from Darwin's aging geology professor Adam Sedgwick, who wrote that he had read the book "with more pain than pleasure. Parts of it I admired greatly, parts I laughed at till my sides were almost sore; other parts I read with absolute sorrow, because I think them utterly false and grievously mischievous."

Harriet Martineau
1802-76

Darwin only took part in such arguments by correspondence, if at all. His ever-present illness kept him from public debates, leaving it to his supporters and opponents to tear at each other in the pages of journals and at meetings of scientists all over the country. Even as Darwin continued with his researches and experiments, *On the Origin of Species* took on a life of its own. Over the years that followed, the strength of its thesis would be put to the test in a new, academic form of the infamous "struggle for survival."

Adam Sedgwick
1785-1873

"A String of Air Bubbles"

IN THE FIVE YEARS AFTER THE PUBLICATION OF ON THE ORIGIN OF SPECIES, OVER 400 BOOKS AND PAMPHLETS WERE PUBLISHED ABOUT IT, ARGUING OVER ITS CONCLUSIONS. ONE OF THE MOST INFLUENTIAL WAS ESSAYS AND REVIEWS, A COLLECTION WRITTEN BY LIBERAL CHRISTIAN THINKERS IN SUPPORT OF DARWIN. HOWEVER, THE BOOK INTRODUCED FRESH CONTROVERSIES TO MANY IN BRITAIN, REVEALING THAT MANY AMONG THE CLERGY WERE ALREADY QUESTIONING THE LITERAL INTERPRETATION OF THE BIBLE.

A review in the *Christian Observer* accepted that selective breeding could produce vast and significant changes in domestic animals, but insisted that this was only possible because God had made it so. Similar variation, it claimed, was not possible in the wild; there was no such thing as "natural" selection. Adam Sedgwick wrote a new angry broadside in the *Spectator*, protesting: "Each series of facts is laced together by a series of assumptions, and repetitions of the one false principle. You cannot make a good rope out of a string of air bubbles." He fought Darwin on a new and unexpected front later in the year, by setting an essay question for the Cambridge University finalists that called upon students to dismiss *On the Origin of Species* as "hypothetical."

Thomas Wollaston, in the *Annals and Magazine of Natural History*, complained that Darwin did not seem to know what a species actually was. The *British Quarterly*, deliberately stirring up trouble, speculated that a time might come when a monkey could propose marriage to a genteel British lady. Perhaps cruelest of all was a cartoon in *Punch* magazine, depicting a gorilla with a sign on its neck. Deliberately evoking the anti-slavery tract of Darwin's Wedgwood forebears, the sign read: "Am I a Man and a Brother?" (See page 109.)

"It is painful to be hated in the intense degree with which — — hates me."

ARISE, SIR CHARLES?

According to the late author Charles Bunting, Darwin was recommended by the prime minister, Lord Palmerston, for the Queen's Honours List in 1860. The recommendation was supposedly quashed by religious advisers, including Samuel Wilberforce, the Bishop of Oxford.

Some biographers have taken this to mean that Darwin lost a potential knighthood through religious enmities. However, Bunting did not supply any documentary evidence for his 1974 claim. Even if it is true, and even considering the explosive impact of the book, it is unlikely that Darwin would have been considered for a knighthood only a month after its publication, although he may have been considered for a lesser decoration.

Lord Palmerston, British prime minister in 1855-8 and 1859-65

"The Londoners say he is mad with envy because my book is so talked about."

"An Abuse of Science"

The review that hurt Darwin the most, however, was an anonymous piece in the *Edinburgh Review*, which ridiculed Darwin and compared him unfavorably to Richard Owen. The piece was soon found to be the work of Owen himself, a man whom Darwin had counted as a friend. Owen had become irritated at the number of Darwin's readers who came to the British Museum and demanded to see "the pigeons," as if the absence of more general natural history exhibits in his crowded galleries was some sort of oversight. More crucially, Owen loathed the very idea of transmutation, and called Darwin's theory an "abuse of science."

"The Londoners," wrote Darwin, "say he is mad with envy because my book is so talked about." He was so angry himself that he refused to name Owen in some letters, instead leaving two dashes.

"Seven Against Christ"

Support for Darwin arrived from an unexpected quarter, with the publication in March 1860 of the volume *Essays and Reviews*, with contributions from seven prominent liberal churchmen. Baden Powell, the Oxford professor of geometry, argued that Darwin's theory left plenty of room for God as a "lawgiver" who set transmutation in motion.

A far more controversial essay was contributed by Benjamin Jowett, the Oxford professor of Greek. Jowett argued that much of the establishment's objection to Darwin was based on antiquated beliefs in the literal truth of the Bible. Although a more allegorical approach had been popular in Germany for years, it was largely unknown to the British public, and caused a storm of controversy.

Essays and Reviews sold even more copies than the early editions of *On the Origin of Species* itself. Its contributors were accused of heresy, and lampooned as "Seven against Christ" in a stinging rebuke by Samuel Wilberforce, Bishop of Oxford, and in a letter to the *Times* signed by the Archbishop of Canterbury and 25 bishops.

"A bench of bishops is the devil's flower garden."

Samuel Wilberforce, the bishop of Oxford, described by Disraeli as "unctuous, oleaginous, saponaceous," leading to his nickname, Soapy Sam.

Darwin's Bulldog

ALTHOUGH DARWIN REMAINED IN RURAL SECLUSION, HIS ARGUMENTS WERE FORCEFULLY CONVEYED TO THE PUBLIC BY HIS STRONGEST AND MOST VOCAL SUPPORTER, THOMAS HUXLEY. A CONVERT TO DARWIN'S THEORY, HUXLEY CHAMPIONED THE CAUSE BEFORE BOTH SCIENTIFIC AND RELIGIOUS CROWDS, GAINING HIMSELF THE NICKNAME "DARWIN'S BULLDOG." IT WAS HUXLEY, NOT THE FRAIL DARWIN, WHO TOOK ON THE MOST SEVERE OPPONENTS OF *ON THE ORIGIN OF SPECIES.*

Thomas Henry Huxley (1825–95) was a scientist after Darwin's own heart. Largely self-taught, the teacher's son was apprenticed to several doctors, before becoming an assistant Surgeon aboard HMS *Rattlesnake*, a Royal Navy vessel on a voyage in the South Pacific that mirrored Darwin's own researches aboard the *Beagle*. On his return, he became a professor of natural science at the Royal School of Mines (now part of Imperial College, London).

The Oxford Debate

One of Huxley's earliest and most notorious performances was in June 1860, at a lively debate held in the Oxford University Museum. No complete transcript of the proceedings exists, although many attendees wrote of its most notorious moments in letters and articles. Hence, many of its most famous arguments or most stinging jibes exist in several different reported forms.

The stars of the opposing sides were Huxley, in favor of Darwin, against Samuel Wilberforce, the bishop of Oxford. Behind the scenes, both had been coached by the true opponents who were absent: Darwin and Richard Owen.

In what appears to have been an unplanned quip, Wilberforce asked Huxley if he thought he was descended from an ape on his father's or mother's side. Huxley retorted that he would rather have simian relatives than claim kinship with a man who used his charisma and authority to quash free debate. Huxley reminded Wilberforce that science flourished on the questioning of authority, and on the testing of proofs, before proceeding to deliver his defense of Darwin's theory.

Huxley's provocative parade of skeletons doubled the size of the gibbon in order to play up its similarities to human beings.

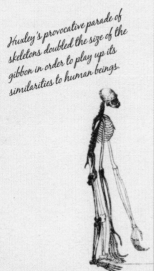

GIBBON   ORANG   CHIMPANZEE   GORILLA   MAN

One of the more surprising attendees was Robert FitzRoy, Darwin's companion for years aboard the *Beagle*, now a civil servant running the Meteorological Department, who had read the book with "the acutest pain." FitzRoy rose to his feet, a Bible held over his head, and proclaimed that the crowd should "believe God rather than man."

Gray Matters

Huxley waged a war of letters and articles against Richard Owen, who had presented a lecture to the Linnean Society arguing that man was separate from all other creatures, because man had unique and specific structures in the brain. Huxley brought up this argument at the Oxford debate, and proved Owen wrong in many subsequent publications. His own book, *Evidence as to Man's Place in Nature*, not only drew powerful links between the brains of apes and humans, but included an iconic frontispiece, in which a line of simian and human skeletons showed obvious similarities—although Huxley deliberately doubled the size of the gibbon to make the connections appear greater than they were.

"Monkeyana," May 1861

Punch Magazine even celebrated the arguments in a poem. Part of it went:

Am I satyr or man?
Pray tell me who can,
And settle my place in
 the scale.
A man in ape's shape,
An anthropoid ape,
Or a monkey deprived of
 his tail?

The *Vestiges* taught,
That all came from naught
By "development," so called,
 "progressive;"
That insects and worms
Assume higher forms
By modification excessive.

Then Darwin set forth
In a book of much worth,
The importance of "nature's
 selection;"
How the struggle for life
Is a laudable strife,
And results in "specific
 distinction."

Let pigeons and doves
Select their own loves,
And grant them a million
 of ages,
Then doubtless you'll find
They've altered their kind,
And changed into prophets
 and sages.

Then Huxley and Owen,
With rivalry glowing,
With pen and ink rush to
 the scratch;
'Tis Brain versus Brain,
Till one of them's slain,
By JOVE! It will be a good
 match!

Says Owen, you can see
The brain of Chimpanzee
Is always exceedingly small,
With the hindermost "horn"
Of extremity shorn,
And no "Hippocampus"
 at all.

Next Huxley replies,
That Owen he lies,
And garbles his Latin
 quotation;
That his facts are not new,
His mistakes not a few,
Detrimental to his
 reputation.

"To twice slay the slain,
By dint of the Brain,
(Thus Huxley concludes
 his review)
Is but labour in vain,
Unproductive of gain,
And so I shall bid you
 'Adieu'!"

The X Club

DARWIN FOUND FURTHER SUPPORT IN THE FORM OF AN UNOFFICIAL DINING SOCIETY OF NINE SCIENTISTS, DEDICATED TO KEEPING RELIGION OUT OF SCIENCE. UNSURPRISINGLY, THEY TOOK EVERY AVAILABLE OPPORTUNITY TO PUSH DARWIN'S IRRELIGIOUS VIEW OF NATURE, AND FROM 1873 TO 1885, AN X CLUB MEMBER WAS PRESIDENT OF THE ROYAL SOCIETY. MEANWHILE, NEW SCIENTIFIC STUDIES ALLOWED DARWIN TO CLAIM NEW SUPPORTERS, EVEN AMONG HIS UNWILLING AND UNWITTING RIVALS.

Thomas Henry Huxley was also the instigator of the new, private dining club, the X Club, whose members were exclusively prominent, anti-religious scientists. Almost all were Fellows of the Royal Society, and their meetings were usually timed to coincide with Society meetings on the same day.

Huxley's intentions were originally an informal monthly dinner, where he could keep up with old friends. The X Club began as a simple agreement that the group would meet once a month at the Albemarle Hotel, London, for a friendly discussion of recent scientific issues. Huxley's dining companions included Herbert Spencer, who coined the term "survival of the fittest," Darwin's sometime neighbor (and former landlord) John Lubbock, and the mathematician William Spottiswoode. Another member was the physicist John Tyndall, who in 1874 would speak publicly about the dismissal of "intelligent design" in the atomic theories of the ancient Greeks.

Darwin, however, was never part of the X Club, although he certainly benefited from the club's support throughout the period when its members were in positions of authority. In one of their earliest coups, the members of the club steered the Royal Society into awarding Darwin the Copley Medal in 1864; the rival nominee was his nemesis, Professor Adam Sedgwick. The president of the Society tempered the controversial decision by specifically stating that Darwin was being honored for his other work—on pigeons, barnacles, orchids, and the like—but most categorically not for his most recent publication.

Darwin, as ever, was too ill to attend, but effusive in his thanks. "I am blessed with many good friends," he wrote to Hooker. "I often wonder that so old a worn-out dog as I am is not quite forgotten."

The X Club's influence waned during the 1890s, when the failure to admit any new blood guaranteed its demise as its original members approached retirement. The club ceased to meet regularly in 1893, after members had moved away, fallen out, or become otherwise occupied.

Darwin's supporters in the X Club met once a month at the Albemarle Hotel, London.

"I am blessed with many good friends … I often wonder that so old a worn-out dog as I am is not quite forgotten."

"*Hardly any recent discovery shows more forcibly than this, how little we as yet know of the former inhabitants of the world.*"

The First Bird

Even Darwin's avowed enemies occasionally offered their support; albeit against their will. Two years after the publication of *On the Origin of Species*, archaeologists in Germany unearthed a 150 million-year-old fossil that they called *Urvogel*, "the first bird." The fossil soon ended up at the British Museum, where Richard Owen classified it as *Archaeopteryx macrura*. Owen, perhaps, had not fully understood the implications, as the "bird" had teeth. Darwin later noted "that strange bird, the *Archeopteryx*, with a long lizard-like tail, bearing a pair of feathers on each joint, and with its wings furnished with two free claws" seemed to be a previously unseen link between dinosaurs and birds; precisely the sort of intermediate stage that helped support his theory of the transmutation of species.

Darwin was unable to resist inserting a mention of the discovery into the third edition of *On the Origin of Species*. By the fourth edition, he was clearly relishing the chance to cite the hated Owen in his own support: "Not long ago, palæontologists maintained that the whole class of birds came suddenly into existence during the eocene period; but now we know, on the authority of Professor Owen, that a bird certainly lived during the deposition of the upper greensand; and still more recently … the *Archeopteryx* … has been discovered…."

The discovery of the *Archaeopteryx* suggested a "missing link" between dinosaurs and birds.

"A Living Grave"

DURING THE MID-1860S DARWIN SUFFERED A STRONG RECURRENCE OF HIS OLD MYSTERY ILLNESS. THIS FORCED A BREAK IN HIS WORK AND SEVERAL MONTHS OF CONVALESCENCE. MEANWHILE, WALLACE OFFERED A NEW APPLICATION OF DARWIN'S THEORY THAT SUGGESTED SOCIETY ITSELF, EVEN MORALS, MIGHT HAVE AN EVOLUTIONARY FUNCTION. DARWIN, HOWEVER, DISLIKED THESE IMPLICATIONS, BOTH FOR SOCIETY AND HIS OWN FAMILY.

Either through the stress caused by the reception of *On the Origin of Species*, or by simple bad luck, Darwin suffered a massive relapse of his illness. His doctor's notes reported "extreme spasmodic daily & nightly flatulence; occasional vomiting … cannot walk above ½ mile – always tired." The simple rocking of a carriage or train would cause Darwin fits of nausea, and he was confined to his bed for months.

He was still bedridden when some terrible news arrived. Passed over for promotion, and in the midst of one of his fits of depression, Robert FitzRoy had finally succumbed to his family curse and taken his own life. Darwin cannot have failed to wonder if *On the Origin of Species*, which caused FitzRoy such "pain," might not have been some small contributor to his old shipmate's fate.

After months without respite, Darwin and Emma traveled to Malvern once more to seek Dr. Gully's treatment. It was the first time they had visited the town since Annie's death, and the couple paid their first visit to their daughter's grave, which they found, overgrown and hidden from view, only after some searching. Darwin's many months away from work, bedridden, poorly, and too weak to even read the newspaper, took their toll on him. When he finally emerged from his convalescence and attended a meeting of a London science society, nobody recognized him. Darwin had allowed a huge, bushy beard to cover his craggy face. The facial hair would stay with him for the rest of his life, and become emblematic of the great man.

Darwin continued to be troubled by the implications that his frail nature held for his children. Annie, he was sure, had died as a result. Her younger sister, Mary, had died when just a month old in 1842. Charles Jr. had died, aged two, of scarlet fever. Henrietta and the boys were all frail, and Elizabeth suffered from some sort of speech impediment or other disorder that left her barely mentioned in Darwin's otherwise voluminous family diaries and correspondence.

"I am now slowly getting up to my former standard. I shall soon be confined to a living grave, and a fearful evil it is."

Darwin tried every possible cure for his unknown illness, but nothing quite worked.

Mutual Assistance

At the Anthropological Society, Alfred Russel Wallace offered a new twist to Darwin's theory. He suggested that the "struggle" between life forms might favor, in some conditions, cooperation between members of the same species in order to ensure the good of the group. Such "mutual assistance" might be found in the division of labor, for example, or in the provision of care for the sick. Wallace wondered if the "moral" nature of European society had allowed it to leap ahead of lesser societies. Ironically, the very same Christian values that divided Darwinians from the Church might have also made Europeans the "fittest" race to conquer the world.

Wallace's argument was couched in terms that would appeal to the Anthropological Society, whose right-wing members enjoyed hearing any thesis that appealed to their sense of cultural superiority. Darwin thought European society was still subject to selection, albeit not the physical characteristics that might hold sway in the world of the "savages."

Instead, Darwin was already musing on new variables, such as sexual selection. "Our aristocracy is handsomer (more hideous according to a Chinese or Negro) than the middle classes, from pick of the women," he wrote to Wallace. Different cultures had different standards of beauty, different concepts of "fitness" for survival. Mutual assistance might help certain individuals in the short term, but did it really help the survival of the race? Civilization had protected Charles Darwin; it had nurtured him and allowed him to come up with a new and interesting idea. But had that idea ultimately killed Robert FitzRoy? Furthermore, would the frail Darwin line bear any grandchildren, or was his lineage already dying out?

The Germ of a New Idea

IN 1868, DARWIN PROPOSED A NEW THEORY DESIGNED TO SUGGEST HOW OFFSPRING MIGHT DIFFER FROM THEIR PARENTS. HE PROPOSED THAT EACH PARENT IN A SEXUAL UNION BROUGHT A NUMBER OF "GEMMULES," OR BUILDING BLOCKS, TO THE LIFE FORM THEY CREATED, AND THAT THESE PACKETS OF INFORMATION WOULD RECOMBINE TO MAKE OFFSPRING MORE OR LESS LIKE THEIR PARENTS. ALTHOUGH FLAWED, THIS IDEA WAS AN EARLY STEP IN THE DEVELOPMENT OF GENETICS.

Darwin was often his own fiercest critic, pushing himself to plug gaps in his hypothesis. *On the Origin of Species* might have described the symptoms of evolution, but Darwin knew that his theory could never be adequately tested until scientists understood its driving force. What was it, for example, that predisposed some of his children to suffer from illnesses, whereas others did not?

In *The Variation of Animals and Plants Under Domestication* (1868), Darwin proposed a possible solution. Scientists already accepted that the cells of the body were able to increase by division at a microscopic level. There was already anecdotal evidence, some of it admittedly crackpot, of the possibility of grafting cells from one animal onto another. Darwin posited that cells had a basic spark of life, a generic building block, which could be adapted to form different parts of a body, such as bone, muscle, or flesh.

Gemmules

However, since every creature grew from a single-celled egg, a blueprint for the final appearance of the fully grown adult would need to be somehow contained within the basic egg. Darwin suggested that there were granules or "gemmules" of cells within all living creatures, and that every part of a body could shed such gemmules. When two creatures mated, their union would bring together random collections of gemmules from the father and the mother. Hence, any offspring would inherit a mixture of characteristics, some from its mother and some from its father.

Darwin was keen to point out that even human embryos seemed to pass through earlier stages of evolution in the womb, first growing and then losing a tail.

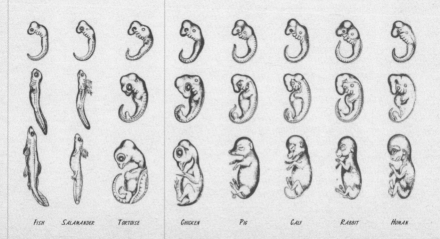

FISH   SALAMANDER   TORTOISE   CHICKEN   PIG   CALF   RABBIT   HUMAN

"They are collected," wrote Darwin, "from all parts of the system to constitute the sexual elements, and their development in the next generation forms the new being; but they are likewise capable of transmission in a dormant state to future generations and may then be developed." In other words, some offspring might seem to take after their grandparents, or even earlier ancestors. Just as is the case when breeding plants or domestic animals, there might be throwbacks to the characteristics exhibited by earlier generations.

Darwin's idea, like that of evolution itself, was not a giant leap in understanding. Nature, as he was fond of saying, did not make giant leaps. Instead, it built on many years of speculation by other scientists about what the building blocks of nature might be. Many had speculated about such things before (including his Edinburgh mentor Grant, who had postulated the existence of atoms of life called "monads"), but Darwin was the first to consider that "gemmules" might constitute packets of information that might be combined or recombined to form a creature. Decades ahead of his time, Darwin had predicted the discovery of DNA.

"These granules may be called gemmules."

GREGOR JOHANN MENDEL (1822–84)

Although Darwin may have believed his idea to be new, it had been pre-empted by the Austrian monk, Gregor Mendel. An experienced beekeeper and gardener, Mendel had experimented with the breeding of hybrid bees and peas, and published a paper on the subject in 1865. However, his work was largely unnoticed until the 20th century, when he became known as the "father of genetics."

Pangenesis

Darwin called his gemmule theory "Pangenesis"; from the Greek for "whole creation," and hoped that later experiments would prove it right. Although it offered a form of explanation for the inheritance of some traits and the discarding of others, as well as for throwbacks (or "atavisms"; from the Latin for a great-grandfather's grandfather), it would later be superseded by the discovery of genes (see Chapter Nine: Darwin's Long-Term Legacy).

Darwin, however was proud of his approach to atavisms, and enjoyed pointing doubters to the way in which developing embryos seemed to undergo transformations as if evolving in the womb from an early, fish-like state, through a reptile stage, and the eventual development of mammalian characteristics. Even human babies seemed to temporarily have tails in the womb, and, indeed, there were some atavisms that retained this tail in adulthood.

The Austrian monk Gregor Mendel's (1822–84) experiments with varieties of peas provided evidence in support of the existence of what we now call genes.

Darwin the Celebrity

AS DARWIN ENTERED HIS SIXTIES HE HAD TO COME TO TERMS WITH HIS NEW-FOUND CELEBRITY, FIGHTING OFF THE UNWELCOME ATTENTIONS OF BOTH ACADEMIC ENEMIES AND AVID FANS. *ON THE ORIGIN OF SPECIES* CONTINUED TO PROPAGATE IN MULTIPLE EDITIONS AND TRANSLATIONS, WHILE DARWIN BOTH UPDATED HIS OLD BOOKS AND PURSUED FURTHER RESEARCHES IN THEIR SEQUELS.

*O*n *the Origin of Species* had secured Darwin's celebrity. Throughout the 1860s and 1870s, he was celebrated and vilified in equal amounts, by an establishment struggling to come to terms with the impact of his ideas. From cartoons in *Punch* to arguments among parliamentarians, Darwin and his ideas were a constant presence.

"The question is," noted the future prime minister Benjamin Disraeli in 1864, "is man an ape or an angel? I am on the side of the angels."

Honors and Accolades

Darwin turned down an honorary doctorate from Oxford (he feared religious opposition), but was made an honorary fellow of Russia's Imperial Society of Naturalists. Prussia had made him a member of its *Orden Pour le Mérite*. The crowning glory of his career was the conferral of an honorary doctorate on him by Cambridge University, his Alma Mater, in 1877. At a raucous occasion attended by a horde of students, including his own son George, Darwin sat through an incomprehensible Latin speech, while student pranksters dangled a stuffed monkey in academic robes from the ceiling. A ring on a string above his head, in a similar fashion, was later understood to be a "missing link."

Benjamin Disraeli, the British prime minister in 1868 and 1874–80 who joked that he was "on the side of the angels."

"is man an ape or an angel?"

Waylaid in Wales

Darwin was not entirely housebound. He pleaded illness to avoid the Oxford dons, but was plainly not too ill to travel to Cambridge. He made occasional excursions to Southampton, Torquay, and London. Sydenham, where Darwin would take the train to London, was also the new home for the Crystal Palace, moved to a nearby hilltop after its one-year sojourn in central London. Darwin made occasional trips to see the exhibits at the Crystal Palace, but was recognized all too often.

He traveled to the west in 1869, stopping off at the Mount to look around his childhood home. Darwin had hoped to wander the grounds alone with his memories, but was mildly piqued that the house's new owners followed him around in awe. North Wales was similarly a disappointment; Darwin had plainly hoped to recall his youth wandering the mountains with a geological hammer, but now could only look longingly at them. Nor did the remote spot offer respite from his fame. Feebly taking a short walk along a country lane, he was waylaid by Frances

Man or Monkey?

As Darwin's fame spread, the most popular aspect of his work with both friends and enemies was the notion of "men from monkeys." The popular press never missed an opportunity to allude to Darwin's supposed kinship with or love of apes. This 1871 caricature of Darwin from the satirical magazine The Hornet *puts the writer's recognizable head on a simian body, and was titled "The Venerable Orang-Outan."*

Power Cobbe, a prominent feminist and animal-rights campaigner he had met at several London events.

Cobbe, who would go on to publish her own work *Darwinism in Morals* three years later, disrupted Darwin's vacation by yelling at him through the bushes that he should read John Stuart Mill's recent *On the Subjection of Women* for some hints on the influence of sexual selection. Not to be outdone, Darwin yelled back that Mill still had a lot to learn about biology, and that it was his own belief that much of men's "vigour and courage" had its origins in evolutionary struggle "for the possession of women." The outdoor debate then ended, with Cobbe shouting after Darwin across the fields that he need to correct his ethical outlook by making a closer reading of Immanuel Kant.

"It is enough to make one wish oneself quiet in a comfortable tomb."

THROUGH THE BRAMBLES

"Mr Darwin was walking on the footpath down from Caer-Deon among the purple heather which clothes our mountains so royally; and impenetrable brambles lay between him and me on the road below; so we exchanged our remarks at the top of our voices, being too eager to think of the absurdity of the situation, till my friend coming along the road heard with amazement words flying in the air which assuredly those 'valleys and rocks never heard' before, or since! When we drive past that spot, as we often do now, we sigh as we look at the 'Philosopher's Path' and wish (Oh how one wishes!) that he could come back and tell us what he has learned since!" — Frances Power Cobbe

CHAPTER EIGHT

DARWIN'S
LATER
WRITINGS

The Descent of Man

IN 1871, DARWIN FINALLY ALLOWED THE OTHER SHOE TO DROP. HIS *DESCENT OF MAN* DIRECTLY ADDRESSED THE ISSUE OF HUMANKIND'S SIMIAN ANCESTRY. HOWEVER, MUCH OF THE TEXT ANSWERED PRE-EXISTING ARGUMENTS, SUCH AS WALLACE'S ASSERTION THAT APES AND HUMANS WERE NOT LINKED, OR THE GROWING DEBATE OVER THE SUPPOSED SUPERIORITY OF CERTAIN RACES.

By the time Darwin published *The Descent of Man, and Selection in Relation to Sex*, the idea that humanity was descended from, as Darwin put it, "some pre-existing form" was by no means new. Many of the readers of *On the Origin of Species* had read between its lines, and the debate on "men from monkeys" had raged for a decade. So *The Descent of Man* was less a statement of a new theory than it was Darwin's defense of certain ideas.

Darwin took pride in his use of the comparison of embryos to show the clear similarities in the development of supposedly different species. *The Descent of Man* also argued with Alfred Russel Wallace, who had begun to swing towards Owen's side of the debate on the simian brain. Even among those scientists who supported Darwin in principle, many simply could not accept the apparently vast gap between the mind of an ape and the mind of a human.

The Woolnerian Tip

In 1868, after five years of pressure from associates, Darwin sat for the sculptor Thomas Woolner. Both were surprised by how well they got along; and while Woolner worked on a bust of Darwin, Darwin quizzed him for an artist's perspective on human expressions.

Woolner revealed in passing that, when working on his 1847 sculpture of Puck, the impish character from *A Midsummer Night's Dream*, he had given the statue pointed ears. "He was thus led to examine the ears of various monkeys, and thus more carefully those of man." Woolner found that a number of humans appeared to have a small bump on the edge of the outermost helix of the ear, which Darwin gleefully identified as the vestige of a simian pointed ear, now folded in on itself. Modern research has suggested that this "Woolnerian Tip," or "Darwin's Tubercle," can be found in as many as 10 per cent of all humans.

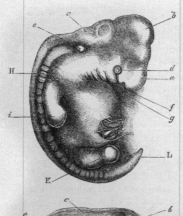

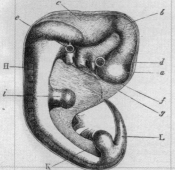

"Excepting in the case of man himself, hardly any one is so ignorant as to allow his worst animals to breed."

Darwin observed remarkable similarities between the embryos of humans (top) and dogs (bottom).

"Nevertheless the difference in mind between man and the higher animals, great as it is, certainly is one of degree and not of kind."

One in ten humans has the Woolnerian lip — the last vestige of an ancestor's pointed ear.

Civilization and Natural Selection

But simple corollaries such as ears were no help in discussing the similarities of actual brains. Darwin also addressed the idea that civilization itself might present an end to natural selection, since it cosseted creatures that would have died out in the natural world. Although most of his readers did not realize, his arguments may have alluded to the work of Thomas Malthus, but he was also thinking of himself.

Darwin wrote *The Descent of Man* in the immediate aftermath of the American Civil War (1861–5), when some anthropologists were arguing that freed slaves would fail to flourish in a free society. But, after his experiences in Tierra del Fuego, Darwin still believed that human races only differed in the most superficial of ways, and that civilization, or savagery, was within the reach of anyone. He was more intrigued by the implications of civilization on the process of natural selection.

"With savages, the weak in body or mind are soon eliminated; and those that survive commonly exhibit a vigorous state of health. We civilised men, on the other hand, do our utmost to check the process of elimination; we build asylums for the imbecile, the maimed, and the sick; we institute poor-laws; and our medical men exert their utmost skill to save the life of every one to the last moment. There is reason to believe that vaccination has preserved thousands, who from a weak constitution would formerly have succumbed to small-pox. Thus the weak members of civilised societies propagate their kind."

The Question of Altruism

Crucially, Darwin argued that sympathy could itself be an instinct that had evolved, whereas a lack of compassion was a mark of savagery. He predicted that civilization would win out over savagery all over the world; a prophecy of moral superiority that has often been misread as a statement of racial superiority. However, for the rest of his life, Darwin was unable to come up with an explanation that truly satisfied him as to how compassion and the care for the weak could form a part of the "survival of the fittest." As with Darwin's ideas on gemmules, further insight on the seeming paradox of altruism would only come after his death (see pages 152–3).

Sexual Selection

THE LATTER HALF OF *THE DESCENT OF MAN* IS DEVOTED TO THE ROLE PLAYED BY SEXUAL SELECTION, A SUBSET OF NATURAL SELECTION IN WHICH COMPETITION OVER MATES AND OFFSPRING LEADS TO CHANGES WHOSE EVOLUTIONARY ROLE IS NOT IMMEDIATELY APPARENT. DARWIN ARGUED THAT STRANGE DEVELOPMENTS SUCH AS THE PEACOCK'S TAIL WERE MIRRORED IN MANY OF THE ATTRIBUTES OF HUMAN SOCIETY. DARWIN WAS PARTIC-ULARLY KEEN TO REFUTE THE CLAIMS OF THE DUKE OF ARGYLL, THAT COLORFUL PLUMAGE AMONG BIRDS WAS THE WORK OF GOD.

Inventing the Horse Before the Cart

In 1867, George Campbell, Duke of Argyll, had published *The Reign of Law*, a book that Darwin found deeply annoying. A supporter of Richard Owen, Campbell argued that while evolution (or "Development") might be observable in the fossil record, it was merely evidence of God's purpose. God, for example, would cause horses and oxen to evolve in time to meet human needs. The brightly colored plumages of birds, Camp-bell went on, were simply God's decorations of nature for humanity's enjoyment.

Campbell added: "Mr Darwin's theory is not a theory on the Origin of Species at all, but only a theory on the causes which lead to the relative success or failure of such new Forms as may be born into the world." Darwin was incensed, regarding Camp-bell's book as an attempt to twist his words, and a deliberate misreading of his theory. Many arguments that Darwin had believed settled were sure to spring up again if he did not deal directly with Campbell's claims.

"The Duke's book strikes me as very well written, very interesting, honest, & clever & very arrogant."

Horns and Tusks

As a result, a huge part of *The Descent of Man* is devoted to Darwin's thoughts on sexual selection; he supplies dozens of examples, in an attempt to curtail the claims of *The Reign of Law*. Darwin took particular interest in the development of long horns on certain species of deer. In the case of the Himala-yan wild goat (*Capra oegagrus*), he reported an observer's account of the way that the male's horns could break its fall if it tumbled from a rocky outcrop. The more docile female, posited Darwin, was less likely to be on the outcrop in the first place, and hence less liable to be favored with long horns.

Tusks and horns, wrote Darwin, were not necessarily part of mating ritu-als; the elephant uses its tusks for many tasks, from scoring the trunks of trees to probing soft ground ahead of itself.

Some horns, however, such as those on the *Oryx leuco-ryx*, seem to have evolved solely for use in the huddled grapple of an oryx mating fight. They bend so far back over

Capra Oegagrus, the horns of which, Darwin believed, served to break a fall.

the animal's head that they would be of little use in fending off predators. They only function when two males hunker down to push and shove each other in competition over a female oryx.

Darwin saw similar sexual selection at work in the preference of female birds for males with ostentatious plumage or particular abilities or attributes. He also saw such selection as evidence of something else: a "high standard of taste" among the females, which suggested that the brains of higher animals were also evolving.

Wallace Disagrees

Alfred Russel Wallace, however, refused to go along with Darwin on matters of sexual selection. He argued that Darwin gave too much credence to the notion that female birds or beetles developed a sense of aesthetics, and was sure that the development of different plumage was itself a form of natural selection. Notably, Wallace also pointed out that Darwin was focusing on the ostentatious end of natural selection. A peacock, for example, might look magnificent to human eyes, but the drab, brown camouflage of the peahen was also a form of natural selection, likely to protect her and her chicks from predators. "It is only in the tropics," noted Wallace, "among forests which never lose their foliage, that we find whole groups of birds whose chief colour is green."

Darwin quoted Wallace's objections in the text of *The Descent of Man* itself, but seemed unable to offer much in the way of refutation. Instead, he was only able to point out the fact that while some birds' plumage had evolved as camouflage, that of others most certainly had not.

Wallace pointed out that brightly colored plumage would actually make some birds easier for predators to spot—hardly a trait that would aid survival.

"We must remember that many parrots are ornamented with crimson, blue, and orange tints, which can hardly be protective."

Savagery and Civilization

DARWIN DEVOTED ONLY THE
LAST THREE CHAPTERS OF
THE DESCENT OF MAN TO
SEXUAL SELECTION AMONG
HUMANS, AND HOW HE
BELIEVED THIS MIGHT HAVE
AFFECTED STANDARDS OF
BEAUTY AND CULTURE AROUND
THE WORLD. HIS VIEWS ON
CIVILIZATION INCORPORATED
CONCERNS ABOUT HIS OWN
FAMILY'S HEALTH, AS WELL AS
A DISPASSIONATE OBSERVATION
OF VICTORIAN NORMS.

Despite the earlier admonitions of Frances Cobbe, Darwin was unafraid to see sexual selection at work in the standards of beauty of Victorian society. He even saw elements of the peacock's tail in a woman's apparent ability to pronounce one man more handsome than another, when the only difference Darwin could see was in the style of his beard.

Darwin noted the obvious, that men tended to be larger and stronger, women smaller and rounder. He found men to be more courageous, hairier, and smarter than women. Darwin posited that many of the norms of Victorian society had their origins in selective processes. Men were steered toward competitiveness, even in the arts, showing off to attract women as peacocks showed off for the benefit of hens. The evolutionary path of women, meanwhile, had steered them toward other, more maternal virtues.

Despite the apparent chauvinism of Darwin's thesis, he was ready to accept that Victorian English norms were anything but universal. He cited several anthropologists on the varying standards of beauty around the world, noting that women in one part of Africa would find a star tattooed on a man's forehead to be an irresistible attraction. Meanwhile, in Manchuria, "a broad face, high cheek-bones, very broad noses, and enormous ears" were considered the height of attractiveness. Darwin noted with interest that "the obliquity of the eye, which is proper to the Chinese and Japanese, is exaggerated in their pictures," seemingly in deliberate contrast with the eyes of Europeans.

In every case, argued Darwin, local custom would favor the offspring of whoever fitted local standards the best. This was a very different definition of the "fitness" upon which survival depended; but nevertheless, it was one that would steer the evolution of certain characteristics among certain races.

"Fanciers always wish each character to be somewhat increased; they do not admire a medium standard."

Dowager Empress Cixi of China, who in her youth was said to be the most beautiful woman in Manchuria. Darwin noted that Manchurian standards were very different from European ones.

"The chief distinction in the intellectual powers of the two sexes is shewn [sic] by man attaining to a higher eminence, in whatever he takes up, than woman can attain—whether requiring deep thought, reason, or imagination, or merely the use of the senses and hands."

Standards of Beauty

"Man scans with scrupulous care," wrote Darwin, "the character and pedigree of his horses, cattle, and dogs before he matches them; but when he comes to his own marriage he rarely, or never, takes any such care." His condemnation of choices in marriage may well have had personal motives. In 1871, the year *The Descent of Man* was published, his daughter Henrietta had married Richard Litchfield, a short, fat local man of whom Darwin did not approve.

Some critics have seen an even more personal message in Darwin's discussion of human mating habits. When he had returned from his *Beagle* voyage, he described himself as a "peacock admiring his own tail," suitable to win the impressionable Emma. Now, decades on, despite his love for his wife, he had begun to question the suitability of their union for providing strong offspring; even the newly married Henrietta was a hypochondriac who had insisted on taking her breakfast in bed ever since she was 13.

Far from arguing for the superiority of humanity, Darwin's book ended with an ironic reversal of the assumption that humans were somehow "better" than their simian ancestors. "He who has seen a savage in his native land will not feel much shame, if forced to acknowledge that the blood of some more humble creature flows in his veins. For my own part I would as soon be descended from that heroic little monkey, who braved his dreaded enemy in order to save the life of his keeper; or from that old baboon, who, descending from the mountains, carried away in triumph his young comrade from a crowd of astonished dogs—as from a savage who delights to torture his enemies, offers up bloody sacrifices, practises infanticide without remorse, treats his wives like slaves, knows no decency, and is haunted by the grossest superstitions."

The Venus de Milo, a statue of the Greek goddess Aphrodite found in 1820, was widely believed to set the European standard of "classical beauty."

The Expression of the Emotions

EVEN *THE DESCENT OF MAN* DID NOT EXHAUST DARWIN'S MATERIALS. A PLANNED CHAPTER ON HUMAN EXPRESSION WAS SET ASIDE TO BECOME AN ARTICLE, YET IT SOON GREW INTO ANOTHER BOOK. ALTHOUGH LARGELY OVERSHADOWED BY DARWIN'S OTHER WORKS, THIS LATEST BOOK WAS INFLUENTIAL ENOUGH FOR THE 20TH-CENTURY SCIENTIST KARL LORENZ TO CANONIZE CHARLES DARWIN AS THE "PATRON SAINT" OF PSYCHOLOGY.

The Expression of the Emotions in Man and Animals was conceived by Darwin as a rebuttal of the work of Charles Bell (1774–1842), who had argued that humankind had been given unique muscles by God to aid in the transmission and creation of emotions. Instead, Darwin suggested that even human emotion was an offshoot of a long evolutionary process, one that incorporated vestiges of animal behavior.

Darwin noted, for example, that the actions of an enraged man "often vaguely represent the act of striking … as when an indignant man unconsciously throws himself into a fitting attitude for attacking his opponent, though without any intention of making an actual attack."

Darwin drew on evidence from questionnaires, but also from personal observation and careful thought about biological imperatives. He noted that the act of screaming would force excess blood into an infant's eyes, and that the muscles around the eye would contract in order to protect the delicate organ. While modern humankind did not scream at every discomfort, the muscles around the eyes were "still less under the control of the will than others," and could cause the eyes to narrow and the forehead to wrinkle when a subject was anxious.

Long before the rise of psychology as an independent discipline, Darwin scoffed at the idea of emotions as learned behavior, noting that even blind people blushed from shame.

Reasoning that a truly instinctual response would be the same all over the world, regardless of race, Darwin drew on evidence from observers of distant ethnic groups, comparing them with his own recollections of the Fuegians whom he had encountered on the *Beagle*. His local experiments extended to sneaky observations of strangers on the train, such as one quiet woman who did not realize that her fellow passenger was intently watching the muscles at the corners of her mouth.

3

4

6

7

The Expression of the Emotions was the first of Darwin's books to use photography to illustrate its points.

"There could now be no doubt that some painful recollection, perhaps that of a long-lost child, was passing through her mind."

— THE EXPRESSION OF THE EMOTIONS, 1872

"An old lady with a comfortable but absorbed expression sat nearby opposite me in a railway carriage. Whilst I was looking at her, I saw that her depressores anguli oris became very slightly, yet decidedly, contracted; but as her countenance remained as placid as ever, I reflected how meaningless was this contraction, and how easily one might be deceived. The thought had hardly occurred to me when I saw that her eyes suddenly became suffused with tears almost to overflowing, and her whole countenance fell."

Questions without Answers

Similarly, Darwin observed that Laura Bridgman, a girl who was both deaf and blind, would clap her hands, laugh and blush when she was happy. Darwin agreed with Herbert Spencer that this might represent some safety valve for excess energy; but he also noted, when tickling the foot of one of his own newborn children, that the limb was instinctively withdrawn. Was laughter, he pondered, a reaction rooted in the contraction of the body to protect it from harm? Or did it have some other purpose, such as the broadcast of satisfaction?

Darwin remained perplexed by laughter and other expressions of joy. He dragged in research from all over the world, noticing that laughter was a feature of the happiness of the Australian aborigines, as well as the Chinese, Hindus, and Malays. He quoted the Greek poet Homer, and his ancient description of Penelope crying with joy when she was reunited with her beloved Odysseus, but could not find a satisfactory explanation.

Darwin's work on *The Expression of the Emotions* coincided with a revised edition of *On the Origin of Species*, and he soon became bogged down. He co-opted two of his children to help him edit the manuscript, but the obvious lack of conclusion and the constant alterations soon left him "sick of the subject, and myself, and the world." He washed his hands of *Emotions*, preferring to conclude with questions for others to ponder. He also presented photographic evidence for the first time, increasing the cost, but not sufficiently to deter its 5,000 buyers.

Despite Darwin's own dissatisfaction, his questions were to form the opening salvos of entire new subsets of later science: sociobiology (the physical origins of social behavior), behavioral ecology (the way in which animals adapt their behavior to suit their environment), and ethology (the scientific study of animal behavior).

As well as members of the public, Darwin also employed professional actors, whose expressions he hoped would be more clearly visible.

Dangerous Plants

Darwin's next set of experiments formed the basis of his book *Insectivorous Plants*. His interest was partly based in the similarities between the "higher plants" and the "lower animals," suggesting that one might have evolved from the other. Darwin experimented on sundews (*Drosora* and *Drosora rotundifolia*) and butterworts, feeding them unusual foods and even poisons to test their reactions. He likened the plants' digestive juices to those of a higher animal's stomach, and began to suspect that insectivorous plants had "nerve matter" that might represent the earliest stages of animal nerves. It was a hypothesis Darwin was keen to test; instead, he faced frustratingly close deadlines, and had to simply speculate.

Books Old and New

Darwin found himself overworked. He wrote in jest that he was on the verge of suicide, faced not only with multiple ongoing book and article deadlines, but also voluminous correspondence and the responsibility of preparing many older books for republication. The very immediacy of Darwin's theories made him eager to insert new passages and citations in order to head off criticism, causing new editions of *On the Origin of Species*, *The Descent of Man*, and *The Variation of Animals and Plants Under Domestication* to balloon with new material.

"I am half killing myself in trying to get a book ready for the press."

Darwin likened the digestive juices of insectivorous plants to those of a higher animal's stomach.

Drosera rotundifolia

Pinguicula vulgaris

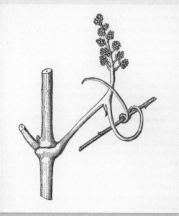

Darwin enlisted the help of his son George, who checked the new editions of a number of books, and provided the illustrations for *The Movements and Habits of Climbing Plants* (1865). Moreover, George also helped Darwin in what at first seemed to be an innocent series of experiments in the pollination of flowers. Plants were kept carefully isolated from insects, so that the Darwins could control every aspect of their propagation. The results, published in *The Effects of Cross and Self Fertilisation in the Vegetable Kingdom* (1876), seemed to prove that crossbred plants were taller, stronger, healthier, and more fertile than "self-fertilised" plants.

The Encouragement of Vice

Darwin, of course, fully intended to put this theory to the test with the human family tree, regarding the inbreeding within his own family and the subsequent illnesses that troubled it as evidence that marriage between cousins led to weaker offspring. George believed that data from lunatic asylums could provide some circumstantial evidence for inbreeding as the cause of mental instability, and the Darwins hoped, in vain, to place a question in the next national census that might give them some statistical material.

It was, however, George, not his father, who bore the brunt of the backlash. Drawing on the research in 1873, George published a brief article in the *Contemporary Review* "On Beneficial Restrictions to Liberty of Marriage." The following year, he was attacked in the *Quarterly Review* by the Catholic thinker St. George Jackson Mivart (1827–1900), who accused him of suggesting "oppressive laws and of the encouragement of vice to check population." Mivart took particular exception to George's advocacy of divorce in certain circumstances, and Darwin was so angry at the attack that he even threatened to change publishers, the *Quarterly Review* being a publication of John Murray.

"This sneer might be easily avoided ... but my advice is to pause, pause, pause."

A sketch of the flower-stalk of a vine by Darwin's son George, from *The Movements and Habits of Climbing Plants*.

DARWIN AMONG THE MACHINES

Samuel Butler's satirical novel *Erewhon*, published in 1872, incorporated pieces of his writing dating back over a decade. Most relevant to the history of evolution was Butler's suggestion, in three chapters under the title "Book of the Machines," that machines might evolve a form of intelligence, and at a faster rate than living creatures. Butler has one character state: "There is no security ... against the ultimate development of mechanical consciousness, in the fact of machines possessing little consciousness now. A mollusk has not much consciousness. Reflect upon the extraordinary advance which machines have made during the last few hundred years, and note how slowly the animal and vegetable kingdoms are advancing."

Some believed Butler's mechanical intelligences to be a satire of Darwin's theory, which he vehemently denied in the preface to its second edition, writing: "Few things would be more distasteful to me than any attempt to laugh at Mr. Darwin."

"Such Rubbish"

DARWIN WAS LEFT UNIM-PRESSED AND IRRITATED BY THE PARLOR TRICKS OF VICTORIAN "MAGICIANS." HIS FIRST ENCOUNTER WITH SPIRITUALISM HAD BEEN AN ILL-ADVISED CONSULTATION WHEN STAYING IN MALVERN, AND HE WROTE IN HIS LETTERS OF HIS CONTEMPT FOR HYPNOTISTS, SPIRITUALISTS, AND HOMEOPATHIC MEDICINES; NONE OF WHICH HE EXPECTED TO STAND UP TO RIGOROUS EXPERIMENTAL ENQUIRY.

"The Lord have mercy on us all, if we are to believe such rubbish."

As a side-effect of Darwin's attitude towards religion, he was far from welcoming of the mid-Victorian fad for spiritualism and parlor magic. As early as 1849, he had scoffed at Dr. Gully's claims that a clairvoyant in Malvern might help diagnose his lifelong illness.

However, after repeated badgering, Darwin eventually agreed to see the woman. True to form, though, he insisted on putting her claims of paranormal abilities to the test. As he arrived, he presented her with a sealed envelope. "I have heard a great deal of your powers of reading concealed writings," said Darwin, "and I should like to have evidence myself: now in this envelope is a banknote—if you will read the number I shall be happy to present it to you."

The clairvoyant scornfully replied that Darwin was asking for a cheap parlor trick, and that she even had a maid at home who could pull off such a deception. Affronted by Darwin's attitude, she wreaked her revenge by describing the awful conditions within his bowels. Darwin was left regarding the entire enterprise as a waste of time, and his physician Dr. Gully as puzzlingly credulous.

Darwin condemned the Victorian fad for spiritualism and séances as nothing more than confidence tricks and parlor games.

"It is a sad flaw, I cannot but think, in my beloved Dr. Gully, that he believes in everything."

Talking Twaddle

By the 1870s, several associates, and even Darwin's brother Erasmus, reported that they had become intrigued by the manifestations of "psychic force" at séances, and wondered if there was some connection to the natural sciences. Perhaps, even, the ghostly images on spirit photographs or the eerie glows that some mediums could summon forth might be evidence of the existence of Darwin's theoretical "gemmules." The concept was certainly enough to intrigue Alfred Russel Wallace, who would eventually publish his thoughts on the subject in a book called *Miracles and Modern Spiritualism* (1896).

Darwin's circle of cynics, however, were less impressed, with Huxley even quipping that the banal nature of so many séances might work as a preventative measure against suicide. "Better to live a crossing-sweeper," he wrote in the *Daily News*, "than die and be made to talk twaddle by a 'medium' hired at a guinea a séance."

A Séance in London

Darwin was invited along with a number of other guests to an afternoon séance at Erasmus's house in 1874, along with Emma, Huxley, and a cluster of Wedgwood cousins, as well Darwin's "half-cousin" Francis Galton. Darwin, it seems, attended not out of scientific curiosity, but because one of the other guests was Marian Evans, better known by her pen-name, George Eliot.

Erasmus and George, Darwin's brother and son respectively, spent over an hour checking the dining room for hidden devices and levers. And the medium, Charles Williams, had agreed to allow them to hold his hands and feet throughout the séance in order to prevent any tricks.

"We had grand fun," noted Darwin sourly, "for George hired a medium, who made the chairs, a flute, a bell and candlestick, and fiery points jump about in my brother's living room, in a manner that astounded everyone and took away their breaths."

However, Darwin only recounted this story second-hand. He had found all the preparations so "hot and tiring", that he excused himself when Williams insisted that the room be plunged into utter darkness. Marian Evans and her husband, who kept making jokes in the dark, also left "in disgust." Huxley and several of Darwin's scientist friends approached the entire enterprise as if it were a puzzle, and they were soon exchanging thoughts on the conjuring tricks that Williams might be employing.

MIDDLEMARCH

George Eliot's *Middlemarch*, first published in serial form in 1871–2, was a favorite of Darwin's. The novel mixed elements that he would have found entertainingly familiar, in particular the character of Edward Casaubon, an aging scholar working on a watershed book in his field, petrified to publish it until it is truly perfect and armored against any dissenting criticism.

Eliot's book, subtitled *A Study of Provincial Life*, also seems to draw, however obliquely, on the notion of the survival of the fittest, as contending family members rise, sink, or remain in place within the changing conditions of their habitat: the British class system.

George Eliot

Endings and Beginnings

DARWIN BECAME A GRAND-FATHER IN 1876. HOWEVER, THIS HAPPY OCCASION WAS TINGED WITH TRAGEDY. THE ARRIVAL OF HIS SON AND GRANDSON AT DOWN TURNED HIS THOUGHTS TO FUTURE GENERATIONS, LEADING HIM TO BEGIN WORK ON THE MOST PERSONAL OF ALL HIS BOOKS, HIS AUTOBIOGRAPHY.

"I know that it would have interested me greatly to have read even so short and dull a sketch of the mind of my grandfather, written by himself."

Thoughts of future generations also turned Darwin's mind to the past, and he began to write his autobiography.

D arwin had been hoping to become a grandfather for some time; Henrietta had remained childless, and Darwin had begun to fret that his offspring were infertile. However, in May 1876, Darwin's son Francis ("Frank") announced that he and his wife Amy were expecting a baby.

For Private Consumption

Elated at the news, Darwin began working on a new, private document: an autobiography intended to be read by his descendants. It was Darwin's intention to give them a glimpse of his life; although much of his usual scientific rigor seems to have eluded him when writing about his own family. The memoirs, written piecemeal from 1876 until shortly before Darwin's death in 1882, constitute only a partial view of their creator. Darwin wrote piously of his dedicated work ethic, but made scarce mention of the illness that gave him little choice but to remain secluded at Down. He wrote his reminiscences of his parents, but painted his father as a bullish, overbearing man, whose most enduring opinion was that Darwin was "good for nothing but shooting, dogs and rat-catching."

There were other revelations. Darwin devoted a long part of his notes to his thoughts on religion, citing observations on the credulous nature of women, but clearly stating his disenchantment with Christianity, as if he feared that the Darwin women would shepherd his descendants back into the religious fold.

Darwin also confessed that his relentless research seemed to have deadened much of his former appreciation for art, music, and literature. "My mind," he wrote, "seems to have become a kind of machine for grinding general laws out of a large collection of facts, but why this should have caused the atrophy of that part of the brain alone, on which the higher tastes depend I cannot conceive."

Settling Scores

Even in a manuscript that was supposedly intended for his family, Darwin couldn't resist attacking those who had misread his work. "As my conclusions have lately been much misrepresented, and it has been stated that I attribute the modification of species exclusively to natural selection, I may be permitted to remark that in the first edition of this work, and subsequently, I placed in a most conspicuous position—namely at the close of the introduction—the following words: 'I am convinced that natural selection has been the main, but not the exclusive means of modification.' This has been of no avail. Great is the power of steady misinterpretation."

"The Most Dreadful Thing"

Darwin's first intended reader, his grandson Bernard Richard Meirion Darwin (1876–1961), was born on September 7. However, the family's excitement soon turned sour when the child's mother, Amy Darwin, contracted some sort of infection shortly after the birth, and died in convulsions just two days later.

> *"It is the most dreadful thing which has ever happened, worse than poor Annie's death, though not so grievous to me."*

"God knows what will become of poor Frank," wrote Darwin, "his life will be a miserable wreck. He is too young to care for the Baby, which must be brought here, & I trust in God we may persuade him to come here & not to live in his house surrounded by memorials of her."

The devastated Frank moved in at Down with his infant son, whom Darwin and Emma thought so solemn that they even joked he might be a reincarnation of some Grand Lama. The only thing that seemed to amuse Bernard was "the sight of his grandfather's face," beard and all. Darwin, for his part, made no attempt at scientific investigations of the baby, but simply enjoyed the presence of a child in the house. The baby's father, however, was another matter, and Darwin tried to drag Frank into various experiments, in order to distract his mind.

EXTINCTIONS

The year of the birth of Darwin's first grandson also saw two of his doom-laden predictions come true.

In the distant Falkland Islands, where Darwin had once pondered the fate of local fauna in the face of the farmers' onslaught, the dog-like warrah was declared extinct. Half way around the world, in what was once called Van Diemen's Land, the authorities noted the death of Truganini, the last of the full-blooded Tasmanian aborigines, whose plight Darwin had observed during the *Beagle*'s brief visit.

The Worms Turn

IN 1880, HUXLEY PRO-CLAIMED THAT *ON THE ORIGIN OF SPECIES*, SOME 21 YEARS AFTER ITS PUBLICATION, HAD "COME OF AGE." DARWIN, HOWEVER, WAS FADING, SHYING AWAY FROM A FINAL BATTLE OVER EVOLUTION, AND DEDICATING HIMSELF TO THE LAST OF HIS WORKS TO BE PUBLISHED IN HIS LIFETIME: BOOKS ABOUT THE EFFECT OF WORMS ON THEIR ENVIRONMENT AND THE MOVEMENT OF PLANTS.

Darwin's grandfatherly musings clearly brought his own grandfather, Erasmus, to mind. When he heard that a German publication in his own honor was to include a long article on the scientist Erasmus Darwin, he arranged to have it translated into English and published as a book. Darwin also hoped that the book would answer new criticisms from Samuel Butler, whose *Evolution Old and New* (1882) had accused Darwin of twisting his grandfather's thoughts on transmutation. He resolved to write the preface himself, but soon had cause to regret the entire enterprise.

Parts of the original article by Ernst Krause turned out not to be original at all; they were not only written in answer to Butler, but lifted whole passages from Butler's work. Other parts, including a direct attack on Butler, had been revised by Krause before translation; Butler had read the original, and accused Darwin of sleight of hand in his publication of a seemingly innocent family biography that still possessed vestiges of an attack on a rival.

With even Emma fulminating at the tone of Butler's "odious and spiteful letter," Darwin prepared for a new battle of words, but eventually took Huxley's advice and met the accusations with silence.

Samuel Butler
1835–1902

"I feel like a man condemned to be hung [sic] who has just got a reprieve."

The Noble Worm

Darwin's last book to be published during his life was *The Formation of Vegetable Mould Through the Action of Worms, with Observations on their Habits* (1881), an unwieldy title often shortened to *Worms*.

Darwin approached the topic with his customary thoroughness, determined to observe the influence of worms not merely on a compost heap over a matter of weeks, but on the earth over thousands of years.

"Solid" earth, as Darwin had known since the South American earthquake in his youth, was anything but. And he devoted an entire chapter to the archaeology of buildings in Silchester near Reading, where the action of worms over centuries had caused tiled floors to break up and stone walls to sink beneath ground level in the old Roman town of Calleva Atrebatum.

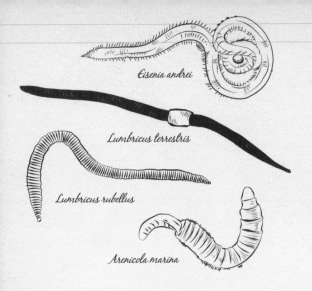

Eisenia andrei

Lumbricus terrestris

Lumbricus rubellus

Arenicola marina

"Archaeologists are probably not aware how much they owe to worms for the preservation of many ancient objects."

"Coins, gold ornaments, stone implements, &c., if dropped on the surface of the ground, will infallibly be buried by the castings of worms in a few years, and will thus be safely preserved, until the land at some future time is turned up." Darwin recalled similar finds of ancient arrowheads in the fields near his native Shrewsbury. They had, he wrote, clearly not lain at the surface all along, but had been churned up by the action of a plow, having presumably been churned down by the action of worms on a battlefield.

A caricature in *Punch* magazine's almanac for 1882 playfully showed humanity (and Darwin) evolving from worms.

Gardeners' Question Time

If Darwin had expected *Worms* to be a minor work, appreciated only by a handful of scientists, he had not counted on the British love of gardening. The book sold in its thousands, generating a volume of correspondence that Darwin found "laughable"; the content of the letters he received ranged from intelligent observations and queries, to crackpot thoughts on Biblical history.

"Among his idiotic letters," wrote Emma to Henrietta, "a good lady writes to ask him whether she may still kill snails, which do her so much damage, or are they as useful as worms. Also a gentleman from Australia to enquire why the blackened and white stumps of trees all about do not affect the colour of the lambs as they did in Jacob's time. I thought he must be joking, but [your father] said he was quite serious."

PUNCH'S ALMANACK FOR 1882.

MAN · IS · BVT · A · WORM.

More Precious Than Rubies

DARWIN DIED, PEACEFULLY, AT DOWN HOUSE SHORTLY AFTER HIS 73RD BIRTHDAY. HIS DEATH IMMEDIATELY SPARKED A NATIONAL ROW, AS HIS SUPPORTERS PETITIONED TO HAVE HIS BODY INTERRED AT WESTMINSTER ABBEY, INSTEAD OF IN THE QUIET CHURCHYARD NEAR HIS HOME. ARGUMENTS FOR A STATE FUNERAL WERE SETTLED BY THE EMBARRASSING REMINDER THAT HIS COUNTRY HAD FAILED TO HONOR HIM IN ANY OTHER MANNER.

Darwin's health, already weak, began to fail more seriously in early 1882. He suffered a seizure while taking one of his turns along the Thinking Path, and could only stumble back, lurching from one tree to the next. His last jottings in his notebook were a dispassionate recitation of his symptoms, as if he were expecting to leap out of bed in a few days and write a paper on angina pectoris syncope, the slow grinding to a halt of a human heart.

Darwin was, however, fading fast, and spent his last three days bedridden, being cared for by Emma, who clearly knew the end was coming, and deliberately spared her husband the final stress of visitations from doctors unable to offer any help.

"It is almost worthwhile to be sick to be nursed by you," he joked to Emma. Perhaps remembering their lifelong opposition on matters of religious belief, and her youthful fretting that he would face damnation unless he found God, he attempted to comfort her, adding: "I am not the least afraid to die. Remember what a good wife you have been."

Darwin lapsed into unconsciousness and died in his wife's arms in the afternoon of Wednesday, April 19, 1882. He was 73.

Our Illustrious Countryman

Darwin had fully expected to be buried in the churchyard in the nearby village of Downe, close to the graves of Mary and Charles, his children who had died in infancy (Annie was buried in Malvern), and his own brother Erasmus, who had died the year before. Emma, it was expected, would eventually join him there.

Darwin's fellow scientists, however, had other ideas. They soon produced a petition, signed by 20 Members of Parliament, that "our illustrious countryman, Mr. Darwin, should be buried in Westminster Abbey."

"Not one of them all has wielded a power over men and their intelligences more complete than that which has for the last twenty-three years emanated from a simple country house in Kent."

— LONDON TIMES

CHARLES ROBERT DARWIN
BORN 12 FEBRUARY 1809
DIED 19 APRIL 1882

London's Westminster Abbey, where Darwin was laid to rest.

DARWIN'S HEIRS: WILLIAM
Darwin's eldest son William (1839–1914) was plagued with similar ill health to Darwin's own, and was forced to give up a promising legal career. He worked in banking in Southampton and caused a stir at his father's funeral by sitting through it with his gloves on his head—his bald spot was cold and he was not permitted to wear a hat inside the Abbey.

Emma was initially reluctant to go against what she had known to be Darwin's wishes, but was talked around by her eldest son. "William felt strongly," she wrote, "and on reflection I did also, that his gracious and grateful nature wd. have wished to accept the acknowledgement of what he had done."

Even as Emma and William debated the right thing to do, the obituaries presented the arguments for them. The *Standard* reported that Darwin would be buried in his country churchyard, but pointedly observed that Westminster Abbey might be more appropriate. Soon, other newspapers began drawing comparisons with the men who had made Britain great. Suggestions that he was the modern Isaac Newton helped make a case for an internment in the Abbey, as did the dawning realization that there was now no other way for his own country to honor him. Although he had received awards equivalent to honorary knighthoods from foreign countries, he had received no similar accolade from his native land. Burying him in the national cathedral at Westminster would be the British establishment's only chance of erasing the contention and controversy that had greeted *On the Origin of Species*, and acknowledging its author's immense contribution to science.

It was eventually agreed by all that Westminster Abbey was the place for Darwin, the sole public complaint being lodged by the landlord of the Downe pub, the George and Dragon, who had been looking forward to some good business from out of town on the day of the funeral.

The pallbearers at Darwin's funeral, on April 26, included the Duke of Argyll, Alfred Russel Wallace, Joseph Hooker, and Thomas Huxley. The lavish ceremony was complete with a specially commissioned funeral hymn, with text taken from the Book of Proverbs. With its talk of joy in the pursuit of knowledge, the passage of eons in the "length of days," and wanderings on a peaceful path, it was perhaps more apt than its composer could have possibly known.

PROVERBS 3:13–17
Happy is the man that findeth wisdom, and the man that getteth understanding. For the merchandise of it is better than the merchandise of silver, and the gain thereof than fine gold. She is more precious than rubies: and all the things thou canst desire are not to be compared unto her. Length of days is in her right hand, and in her left hand riches and honor. Her ways are ways of pleasantness, and all her paths are peace.

CHAPTER NINE

DARWIN'S LONG-TERM LEGACY

A World without Darwin

FOR A WHILE, IT SEEMED AS IF DARWIN'S THEORIES WOULD SLOWLY DIE OUT, SWAMPED BY RESURGENT ARGUMENTS FROM SUPPORTERS OF DIVINE INFLUENCE, LAMARCKIANS, AND BELIEVERS IN SUDDEN CHANGE RATHER THAN THE SLOW PROCESS OF NATURAL SELECTION. IT TOOK FOUR DECADES FOR DARWIN'S THEORIES TO FUSE WITH GENETICS TO CREATE THE "MODERN EVOLUTIONARY SYNTHESIS."

Scientists continued to speculate over what led the combination of a sperm and egg to produce a new life form.

Huxley's grandson, Julian, would write decades later of the "eclipse of Darwin," as the fading memory of Darwin, and the aging of his most vehement supporters, left the field open for a resurgence of opponents.

Even if evolution was an agreed element of biology among natural scientists, there was still intense disagreement over the engine of evolution. Darwin's concept of natural selection was one of many contending possibilities, and was briefly hidden by other ideas.

Theistic Evolution

The idea espoused by the Duke of Argyll, Mivart, and many others, that God set evolution in motion and steered its direction, gained sway once more in the late 19th century. Darwin himself had not ruled out the possibility of a "First Cause"— some unknown creative force that had made the universe—but saw no need to believe in the Bible, the Christian God, nor any other belief system. Theistic evolution lacked any means of proof, and was impossible to locate within the scientific method; how does one prove that a random event is actually part of "God's plan"?

Intracellular Pangenesis

The Dutch biologist Hugo de Vries (1848–1935) drew on Darwin's theory of gemmules for his own work, *Intracellular Pangenesis*, in 1889. In it, de Vries argued that living organisms possessed particles, or "pangenes," that contained the information necessary to make other living organisms. He attempted to prove this, much as Darwin had done, by experimenting on the hybridization of plants, in particular the evening primrose. De Vries also believed that the pangenes could cross between species.

De Vries rediscovered the work of Mendel in the 1890s, and by 1900, two other biologists had pointed out the similarities between the theory of pangenes and Mendel's work. A generation later, pangenes became better known as genes.

Hugo de Vries whose theory of "pangenes" temporarily supplanted Darwin's.

The Weismann Barrier

August Weismann (1834–1914) also drew on Darwin's theory of gemmules, suggesting that there might be some form of "germ plasm" in the cells that form new life: eggs and sperm. Weismann argued that "somatic cells," that make the rest of a living organism, were formed by germ cells, but could not influence them. Although the notion of germ plasm has been disproved, the idea that heredity was a one-way street would become an important concept in post-Darwinian biology. In other words, a creature could not pass on characteristics it had acquired during its life to its offspring. This ruled out the inheritance of acquired characteristics, and hence led Lamarckian theories to fall out of favor.

August Weismann (1834-1914)

Saltationism

Whereas Darwin had claimed that "nature does not make a jump," other biologists were happy to think that it did. The "saltationists," including de Vries, argued that nature could indeed make massive leaps, through mutation brought about by radiation from cosmic rays and other influences. Thomas Hunt Morgan (1866–1945) set out to prove this by experimenting on populations of fruit flies, steering mutations with careful selection of mating choices, and exposing them to radiation and chemicals. To his surprise, he found himself proving quite the opposite.

As Darwin had noted 60 years earlier, in his observations of the Mauchamp-merino sheep, breeders often fixated on one deviation that was important to them, and ignored those that accompanied it. While attempting to breed white-eyed fruit flies instead of red-eyed fruit flies, Morgan found a small wing mutation that was passed on separately. His own data led him to conclude that evolution proceeded in tiny increments, not great leaps, and that the increments were discrete units. It was another argument in favor of both the existence of genes and natural selection.

WHY FRUIT FLIES?

Morgan and many other geneticists favored the humble fruit fly (*Drosophila melanogaster*) because of the speed with which its generations pass. Females are ready to mate within just hours of hatching, and a "generation" of fruit flies passes in around 10 days, rather than the 20 years of humans.

The fly also has several readily identifiable characteristics and a small number of chromosomes, making it easier to track changes in its appearance and genetic make-up. In modern times, fruit flies are particularly useful because 75 per cent of human genes are matched in the fruit fly's genome, and they can be used to test elements of human diseases, such as cancer and diabetes.

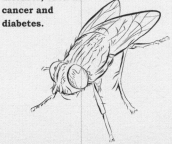

A Deathbed Conversion?

DARWIN'S AUTOBIOGRAPHICAL FRAGMENTS WERE PUBLISHED FIVE YEARS AFTER HIS DEATH, ALBEIT WITH SOME OF THEIR MORE CONTROVERSIAL COMMENTS ABOUT RELIGION OMITTED. WHEN AN AMERICAN MAGAZINE PUBLISHED A STORY SUGGESTING THAT DARWIN HAD RECANTED ON HIS DEATHBED, TWO OF DARWIN'S CHILDREN RUSHED TO DENY IT. HOWEVER, IT TOOK SEVERAL DECADES FOR DARWIN'S TRUE THOUGHTS TO SURFACE IN AN UNABRIDGED VERSION OF HIS AUTOBIOGRAPHY.

Darwin's own wealth, combined with that of his brother Erasmus, who had died without issue, left the value of his estate at something approaching a quarter of a million pounds, a fortune in the 19th century, and sure to leave his heirs well-off. Darwin's publications continued after his death, with his name appearing on several papers and letters. Emma Darwin lived on until 1896, and several of her children appear to have colluded in an effort to protect her Christian sensibilities from any public revelations about her husband's attitude toward religion.

Darwin's Heirs: Frank and Etty

Francis (Frank) Darwin (1848–1925) was a natural scientist, albeit of a minor caliber compared to his father. His greatest discovery, co-published with his father in *The Power of Movement in Plants*, was that seedlings directed the growth of their sprout toward a light source. Five years after Darwin's death, Frank edited *The Life and Letters of Charles Darwin*, incorporating pieces of his father's autobiography. However, Frank and his mother had agreed to remove much of Darwin's private thoughts on religion, which were distressing to them and liable to cause controversy elsewhere.

Frank Darwin

Darwin Defended

When Lady Hope (see box) published the allegation that Darwin was a devout Christian, Francis wrote a rebuttal in 1918, calling her story "quite untrue." However, despite his answer, and what would have been a shockingly direct accusation that her words were "falsehood," the story continued to flourish. It was left to another of Darwin's children to quash it in the year of Lady Hope's death.

Henrietta ("Etty") Darwin (1843–1929), who had married Robert Litchfield, had helped her father edit some of his later books, and would later edit *Emma Darwin, Wife of Charles Darwin: A Century of Family Letters* (1904). When the Lady Hope story resurfaced in 1922, the aging "Mrs R.B. Litchfield" wrote a stern response for *The Christian* magazine: "I was present at his deathbed, Lady Hope was not present during his last illness, or any

---

HOPE'S HOAX

In 1915, Elizabeth Reid, also known as Lady Hope, wrote an article for the American Baptist newspaper, the *Watchman Examiner*, in which she claimed to have visited Darwin shortly before his death, and spoken with him about the Bible, which she claimed to have found him reading.

She went on to claim that Darwin loved the Bible, begged her to give a sermon on "Christ Jesus and his salvation," and spoke of his wish to recant his theories.

"I was a young man with unformed ideas," Darwin supposedly said. "I threw out queries, suggestions, wondering all the time over everything, and to my astonishment, the ideas took like wildfire. People made a religion of them."

illness. I believe he never even saw her, but in any case she had no influence over him in any department of thought or belief. He never recanted any of his scientific views, either then or earlier."

Darwin's Heirs: Horace and his Children

The story of the Hope allegation continued through another generation of Darwins. The youngest son, Horace (1851–1928), became the proprietor of a scientific instrument company. Of his three children, the eldest, another Erasmus, was killed at the Second Battle of Ypres in 1915. The next, Ruth Rees-Thomas, married a proponent of the growing eugenics movement. And the youngest, Nora Barlow, would become the editor of a new version of Frank's *Life and Letters*, published in 1958 to mark the centennial of the publication of *On the Origin of Species*.

Barlow's version of the manuscript restored those passages that had been cut by her uncle, on the understanding that most of those who might have been wounded by them were now dead. Furthermore, Barlow considered Darwin's own words to be the best defense against attempts by the likes of Lady Hope to imply he had undergone some sort of deathbed conversion.

Darwin's grandson Erasmus was killed in the First World War at the Second Battle of Ypres, a terrible landmark in the "evolution" of military might.

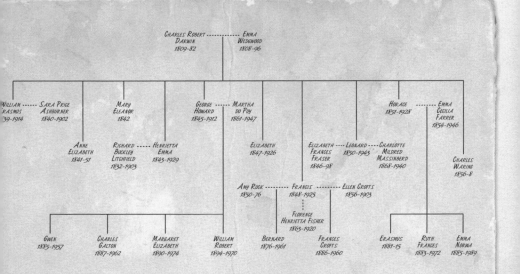

CHARLES ROBERT DARWIN 1809-82 ------ EMMA WEDGWOOD 1808-96

WILLIAM ERASMUS 1839-1914 ------ SARA PRICE ASHBURNER 1840-1902

MARY ELEANOR 1842

GEORGE HOWARD 1845-1912 ------ MARTHA DU PUY 1861-1947

HORACE 1851-1928 --------- EMMA CECILIA FARRER 1854-1946

ANNE ELIZABETH 1841-51

RICHARD BUCKLEY LITCHFIELD 1832-1903 ----- HENRIETTA EMMA 1843-1929

ELIZABETH 1847-1926

ELIZABETH FRANCES FRASER 1846-98 ---- LEONARD 1850-1943 ---- CHARLOTTE MILDRED MASSINGBERD 1868-1940

CHARLES WARING 1856-8

AMY RUCK 1850-76 --------- FRANCIS 1848-1925 --------- ELLEN CROFTS 1856-1903

FLORENCE HENRIETTA FISHER 1863-1920

GWEN 1885-1957

CHARLES GALTON 1887-1962

MARGARET ELIZABETH 1890-1974

WILLIAM ROBERT 1894-1970

BERNARD 1876-1961

FRANCES CROFTS 1886-1960

ERASMUS 1881-15

RUTH FRANCES 1883-1972

EMMA NORNA 1885-1989

The Missing Links

AFTER DARWIN'S DEATH, NEW DISCOVERIES IN THE FOSSIL RECORD POINTED TO SEVERAL INTERMEDIATE STAGES IN THE DEVELOPMENT OF HUMANKIND. JUST AS *ARCHAEOPTERYX* HAD SUGGESTED TO DARWIN A LINK BETWEEN DINOSAURS AND BIRDS, SEVERAL EARLY HOMINIDS SUGGESTED A SIMILAR DEVELOPMENT OF MODERN HUMANKIND FROM APES. AS DARWIN HAD PREDICTED, THE FOSSIL RECORD BEGAN TO SUPPORT HIS THEORY.

The Dutch explorer Eugène Dubois (1858–1940) set out in search of a missing link that might prove Darwin's hypothesis. Finding a piece of skull and a leg bone in Java, he called his discovery *Pithecanthropus erectus* ("an upright ape-man"). Subsequent finds, of "Peking Man" at Zhoukoudian in China, led many biologists in the early 20th century to assume that Darwin had been incorrect in his assumption that humanity's origins lay in Africa. However, the idea of an Asian origin has gradually dwindled in the face of ever-growing evidence of even older ancestors from Africa.

The Laetoli Footprints

In 1978, the archaeologist Mary Leakey discovered a set of fossilized footprints in Laetoli, Tanzania. They appear to have been made by a family of hominids fleeing a volcanic eruption, and were preserved by the action of the ash that later fell on the prints and filled them in. The spacing and size of the footprints allowed her to gauge the figures' height, weight, and gait; they had been walking upright at a leisurely pace.

Survival of the Fittest?

Darwin was aware in his own lifetime of the discovery of the skulls of primitive hominids in the valley of Neanderthal, in Germany, in 1856.

The discovery was pronounced to be *Homo neanderthalensis*, although earlier discoveries elsewhere in Europe were later proclaimed to be examples of the same species. Hairy, with prominent brows and a sloping forehead, Neanderthals were thought to be tool-using creatures, regarded by evolutionists in Darwin's time as a possible early stage in humankind's development. However, debates over Neanderthals have raged up until the present day, constantly altered by new discoveries, speculations, and genetic mapping.

The Laetoli footprints represent some of the earliest evidence of hominids walking upright.

"We ought to look for a few links, some more closely, some more distantly related to each other"

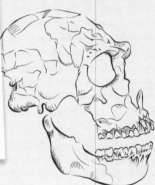

Louis and Mary Leakey, in 1959, hold a skull estimated to be 600,000 years old. Scientists came to believe that human evolution was centered in Africa rather than Asia.

"In Madagascar there must be moths with probosces capable of extension to a length of between ten and eleven inches!"

Several of the early hominids in the fossil record appear to have died out before or during the rise of the modern human (*Homo sapiens*; "wise human"). Some varieties of *Homo erectus* endured until only 100,000 years ago, and the Neanderthal appears to have lived alongside *Homo sapiens* in some locations.

The fate of the Neanderthals remains unknown. Speculation that the species may have been sufficiently closely related to *Homo sapiens* for the two groups to interbreed has yet to be proved through DNA research. Instead, the evidence currently suggests quite the opposite, that Neanderthals were either wiped out by the relative newcomers, or died out in isolated communities that avoided all possible contact with the new arrivals.

MORGAN'S SPHINX

In his book *On the Various Contrivances by which British and Foreign Orchids are Fertilised by Insects, and on the Good Effects of Intercrossing* (1862), Darwin noted that a Mr. Bateman had sent him several samples of the Madagascar star orchid, a flower whose nectar was tucked so far out of harm's way that it would have taken a moth with an 11-inch (28-centimeter) proboscis to get at it. Darwin predicted that, if his theory of natural selection held, such a moth would eventually be discovered, however unlikely it might sound, as otherwise the orchid would have no way of pollinating. Sure enough, in 1903, such a moth was found, and named *Xanthopan morgani praedicta* ("Morgan's Sphinx, as predicted").

Peking man, whose remains were discovered in the early 20th century, is another possible intermediate stage between apes and humans.

Social Darwinism

A NUMBER OF EUROPEAN THINKERS, PARTICULARLY THE ARDENT ZOOLOGIST ERNST HAECKEL, BEGAN TO DEBATE THE EFFECT OF DARWIN'S THEORIES ON HUMAN SOCIETY. IF FORTUNE FAVORED THE FITTEST, WHAT WAS "FITTEST" FOR SOCIETY? THE DEBATES SOON LED DOWN A DANGEROUS ROAD TOWARD NOTIONS OF RACIAL SUPERIORITY. WHERE DARWIN HAD EMPHASIZED THE SIMILARITIES BETWEEN MODERN HUMAN RACES, HIS COUSIN FRANCIS GALTON BEGAN TO DWELL ON THE DIFFERENCES.

Ernst Haeckel (1834–1919) was sometimes called the "German Darwin." During Darwin's life, Haeckel's classes in "Darwinismus" at the University of Jena had attracted 150 students at a time, and encouraged a generation of European scientists to honor Darwin with a degree of respect still contested in Darwin's home country.

Vetted by Huxley and pronounced worthy, Haeckel had been one of the rare guests to visit Darwin at Down House, where the two men had jabbered at each other excitedly, neither really understanding the other's language, to their great amusement, and to Emma Darwin's great irritation.

Recapitulation

Haeckel proposed in 1866 that the development of an embryo in the womb would "recapitulate" the development of a species, showing elements of the ancestor-species from which it had evolved: fish, reptiles, lower mammals, and so on. In Darwin's autobiography, he would grumble mildly about Haeckel's "discovery," which he believed he had made himself in the earlier *On the Origin of Species*.

Recapitulation became part of Haeckel's theory that humankind itself had lower and higher orders and that Haeckel's own race, the white European, occupied a superior branch on the tree of life to, say, that of the black African. However, recapitulation is widely discredited in modern times. Embryos might show elements of earlier species, but do not pass through distinct stages equivalent to their development.

Regardless, Haeckel's theory was soon put to another use, in suggesting that biology determined social position. If white culture and white civilization were considered "superior," then it followed that no social, financial, or educational remedy could rescue "lower races" from their biological inferiority.

AFRICA FOR THE CHINESE: A MODEST PROPOSAL?
"My proposal is to make the encouragement of the Chinese settlements ... on the East Coast of Africa a part of our national policy, in the belief that the Chinese immigrants would not only maintain their position, but that they would multiply and their descendants supplant the inferior Negro race. I should expect the large part of the African seaboard, now sparsely occupied by lazy, palavering savages ... might in a few years be tenanted by industrious, order loving Chinese, living either as a semi-detached dependency of China, or else in perfect freedom under their own law."
— FRANCIS GALTON, LETTER TO *THE TIMES*, JUNE 5, 1873

HAECKEL REMEMBERS

"When the carriage drew up before Darwin's house, with its ivy and its shadowy elms, the great scientist stepped out of the shade of the creeper-covered porch to meet me. He had a tall and venerable appearance, with the broad shoulders of an Atlas that bore a world of thought: a Jove-like forehead ... with a lofty and broad vault, deeply furrowed by the plow of intellectual work. The tender and friendly eyes were overshadowed by the great roof of the prominent brows. The gentle mouth was framed in a long, silvery-white beard. The noble expression of the whole face, the easy and soft voice, the slow and careful pronunciation, the natural and simple tenor of his conversation, took my heart by storm in the first hour that we talked together, just as his great work had taken my intelligence by storm at the first reading. I seemed to have before me a venerable sage of ancient Greece, a Socrates or an Aristotle."

— ERNST HAECKEL

A plate from Ernst Haeckel's beautiful *Kunstformen der Natur* ("*Artforms of Nature*").

Nature vs. Nurture

Darwin's cousin, Francis Galton, began enquiries on similar lines. Asking whether intelligence and abilities could be inherited by later generations, he began experiments into the question of whether character was created by nature (inherited), or by nurture (learned). Galton published *Hereditary Genius* (1869), in which he speculated on how many offspring followed in their fathers' illustrious footsteps. He followed in 1874 with the results of a questionnaire he had distributed among members of the Royal Society, and *The History of Twins* (1875), pioneering the use of identical twins in behavior genetics—in such cases, the nature is identical, only nurture is different.

Shortly after Darwin's death, Galton published *Inquiries into Human Faculty and Its Development* (1883), in which he concluded that nature was more influential than nurture. Since, in Galton's view, the best humans bred later and less often, he advocated that society should develop a points system that offered incentives for those of the best racial stock to have more offspring. This, he thought, would avoid dysgenics, or bad breeding. He even coined a new term for its "good" opposite: eugenics.

Francis Galton (1822–1911) wrote a novel, *Kantsaywhere*, about a utopia where only the fittest were permitted to breed. Only fragments survive today.

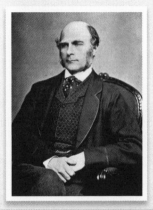

Eugenics

**DESPITE DARWIN'S CAUTION-
ARY NOTE THAT "SYMPATHY"
WAS ONE OF THE HIGHER
TRAITS OF HUMAN EVOLUTION,
THE EARLY 20TH CENTURY
SAW HIS IDEAS TWISTED IN
AN OMINOUS DIRECTION.
ORGANIZATIONS IN MANY
COUNTRIES BEGAN TO
PROMOTE THE CONCEPT
OF RACIAL "PURITY" AND
STRENGTH, WHICH LED
TO GOVERNMENT PROGRAMS
IN SEVERAL INSTANCES, MOST
NOTORIOUSLY NAZI GERMANY.**

The eugenics movement found support all over the world. In the United States, Alexander Graham Bell published the results of his own investigations into congenital deafness in Martha's Vineyard, concluding that two deaf parents were more likely to have deaf children. He subsequently recommended that partners with matching disabilities should be discouraged from marrying.

From 1910, the Eugenics Record Office (ERO) monitored many family pedigrees, leading to state programs aimed at preventing the immigration of "undesirables," the mixing of races, and the marriage of individuals whose heritage was thought to point toward "unfit" children. American eugenics generally favored the "Nordic" races, citing those of Eastern European, black African, and Asian heritage as undesirable. In an additional move adopted by some states, a sterilization program sought to prevent "inferior" people from breeding.

Ironically, just as Darwin had refused to recognize any significant variation between races beyond the most cosmetic differences in skin color, the ERO's statistics also suggested that financial and social background were far more likely to influence criminal behavior than genetic heritage. Regardless, eugenics programs ensued in many other countries, although their implied endorsement of abortion and contraception ensured that few Catholic countries became involved.

In Australia, half-aborigine children were taken from their parents in the hope they might be raised "white." In Canada, the sterilization of "mentally deficient" citizens was legal until 1972. Nor was eugenics limited to Europe or European colonies; in Japan, similar rules were forced upon habitual criminals and sufferers from some mental illnesses and congenital conditions.

"Among the Spartans all newly born children were subject to a careful examination or selection. All those that were weak, sickly, or affected with any bodily infirmity, were killed. Only the perfectly healthy and strong children were allowed to live, and they alone afterward propagated the race."

— ERNST HAECKEL

The children of partisan parents from Celje (now in Slovenia), arrive in Frohnleiten, Austria, where they are met by German military police officers, August 1942. The children, classed as "racially desirable," are being relocated and placed in children's homes or with foster parents, where they can be indoctrinated with Nazi ideology.

Darwin's Heirs: Leonard

Darwin's son Leonard (1850–1943) was an enthusiastic proponent of Galton's theories. A former military man and sometime scientist, he succeeded Galton as the chairman of the Eugenics Education Society, presiding from 1911 to 1928, by which time the name had been changed to the Eugenics Society. Ironically, Leonard considered himself to be the least intelligent of Darwin's children, and married his own cousin. However, although there were supporters of eugenics in the United Kingdom, it never became the subject of government programs.

The Master Race

Eugenics found its most infamous incarnation in Germany, during the years when Adolf Hitler and the Nazi party held power. Hitler believed that the German "master race" risked dilution and diminishment through interbreeding with *untermenschen*, the "under races." And he attempted to arrest this process with a twin-pronged attack: "positive eugenics," which sought to promote desirable characteristics; and "negative eugenics," which sought to eliminate undesirable ones.

Nazi Germany offered incentives to the parents of children with approved racial characteristics, and infamously carried out the extermination of millions of Jews, Poles, Gypsies, homosexuals, and other "undesirables."

Reconsideration and Redemption?

In the aftermath of the Second World War, eugenics policies were largely discredited and repudiated, leading to the United Nations Universal Declaration of Human Rights in 1948. Huxley's grandson, Julian, observed that the horror of Nazi Germany would mean "any radical eugenic policy will be for many years politically and psychologically impossible." He allowed, however, that the philosophy of eugenics was sure to recur in the future.

"It is very difficult to say why one civilized nation rises, becomes more powerful, and spreads more widely, than another; or why the same nation progresses more quickly at one time than at another. We can only say that it depends on an increase in the actual number of the population, on the number of the men endowed with high intellectual and moral faculties, as well as on their standard of excellence. Corporeal structure appears to have little influence, except so far as vigour of body leads to vigour of mind."
— *The Descent of Man*, 1882

Evolution vs. Religion

THE STAND-OFF BETWEEN EVOLUTIONARY THEORY AND RELIGIOUS DOGMA PERSISTS TO THIS DAY. A FAMOUS TRIAL IN 1925 POINTED TO CONTRADICTIONS BETWEEN THE TEACHING OF RELIGION AND SCIENCE IN SCHOOLS. IN THE MODERN AGE, THERE ARE STILL THOSE WHO REFUSE TO CONTRADICT A SINGLE WORD OF THE BIBLE, EVEN THOUGH THE BIBLE CONTRADICTS ITSELF. OTHERS PUSH FOR AN EVOLUTIONARY THEORY THAT RECOGNIZES THE EXISTENCE OF GOD, CONTRARY TO DARWIN'S OWN ASSERTIONS.

Creationists believe in the literal truth of the Bible: that God created the universe in six days, and all the creatures were placed on the Earth at that time, fully formed. In fact, the 1925 Butler Act in Tennessee made it illegal to teach "any theory that denies the story of the Divine Creation of man as taught in the Bible, and to teach instead that man has descended from a lower order of animals."

This new statute was soon tested in a trial when a local high-school teacher, John Scopes, claimed that he had broken the law by teaching Darwin's theory of evolution. Legal debates proceeded for several days on the matter of whether the Bible was true, notably with the counsel for the defense, Clarence Darrow, putting the prosecutor William Jennings Bryan in the dock and cross-examining him about his knowledge of the Bible and of other faiths.

"You insult every man of science and learning in the world," argued Darrow, "because he does not believe in your fool religion." When questioned as to the relevance of his questioning, Darrow proclaimed that he aimed to prevent "bigots and ignoramuses from controlling the education of the United States."

With the judge excluding religious debate from the record, the jury was obliged to find a guilty verdict, since Scopes himself had claimed to have broken the law in question. Scopes was fined a nominal $100, but did not pay it, as the case was overturned on a technicality. The Butler Act, however, remained on the Tennessee statute books until 1967, and the teaching of evolution remains a controversial topic in some American communities, even those that accept its existence.

Intelligent Design

Darwin's theory of evolution has also come under attack in modern times by advocates of "intelligent design," the return of the concept that evolution had been somehow steered by a divine agent. The idea was one that Darwin had repudiated during his own lifetime: "The old argument of design in nature ... which formerly to me seemed so conclusive, fails now that the law of natural selection has been discovered. We can no longer argue that, for instance, the beautiful hinge of a bivalve

John T. Scopes (1900–70) was a school football coach who claimed to have mentioned natural selection when filling in for an absent fellow teacher.

> *"I have discussed this subject at the end of my book on the Variation of Domestic Animals and Plants, and the argument there given has never, as far as I can see, been answered."*

shell must have been made by an intelligent being, like the hinge of a door by man. There seems to no more design in the variability of organic beings … than in the course which the wind blows."

The arguments of the intelligent design lobby were largely answered within Darwin's own works. However, a newer contention is that the universe must have been "fine-tuned" by its Creator in order to make life possible. Such an argument, however, can only ever be self-referential. It is not proof of the existence of a Creator, merely a statement that life as we know it exists within the limits that we know.

One controversial new debate centers on Darwin's thoughts on "inimitable perfection" (see page 97). Although Darwin believed that he had demonstrated evolution very well by breaking down the complexities of the human eye, some modern advocates of intelligent design suggest that the construction of the universe at a sub-atomic level is so unknowable and unpredictable that, if Darwin were alive today, he would regard it as "inimitable," and therefore as the refutation to his theory that he had previously invited. Even this, however, does not disprove natural selection; at most it would merely be evidence to offer in favor of the existence of a "First Cause," something that Darwin never denied, although many others have.

Edward O. Wilson, in the afterword to a 2006 edition of Darwin's most famous books, noted only half in jest that supporters of intelligent design would be welcomed, praised, indeed fêted by the scientific establishment if they could simply demonstrate it at work. "Any researcher who can prove the existence of intelligent design within the accepted framework of science will make history and achieve eternal fame. He will prove at last that science and religious dogma are compatible."

Defenders of intelligent design continue to argue that the universe shows evidence of it, in the same way that the intricacies of a watch imply a watchmaker. But Darwin himself could find nothing in nature that could not be explained by natural selection.

The Selfish Gene

MODERN DEVELOPMENTS IN BIOLOGY CONTINUE TO REFINE AND REINTERPRET OUR UNDERSTANDING OF DARWIN'S IDEAS. THE CLASSIFICATION OF DNA HAS ALLOWED THE DISCOVERY OF INDIVIDUAL BUILDING BLOCKS OF LIFE; AND WE ARE EVEN BEGINNING TO UNDERSTAND THE FIELDS OF GENE THERAPY AND GENETIC ENGINEERING.

In 1869, the Swiss researcher Friedrich Meischer examined pus from surgical bandages under a microscope, and identified a microscopic substance within the nucleus of a cell. He named this material "nuclein." It was another 50 years before nuclein was broken down into its components, and it was not until 1937 that X-rays identified its structure. In 1953 James D. Watson and Francis Crick, using evidence gleaned during X-ray studies by Maurice Wilkins and Rosalind Franklin, established that Meischer's "nuclein" was part of a vast sequence of nucleic acids, a chain of information that essentially formed the data to create an entire life form.

Now known as deoxyribonucleic acid (DNA), these chains are understood to be the basic building blocks of life, which recombine in sexual reproduction to create variation between parents and offspring. It was not quite the realization of Darwin's "gemmules" from 85 years earlier, but it was pretty close.

The Human Genome

Starting in the 1970s, modern bioscientists have attempted to map the entire sequence of DNA "programing" that forms a human being. This involved establishing which pieces of DNA correspond to which traits in a life form. As each element is pinned down, it becomes possible to replicate or alter particular pieces of the gene, making it possible to alter certain characteristics before birth; changing eye color, for example, or removing a susceptibility to a particular disease.

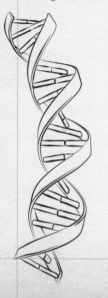

The distinctive double helix of DNA, the building block of life.

"It is, perhaps, not too bold a supposition that unmodified and undeteriorated gemmules of the same nature would be especially apt to combine."

Altruism Answered

The evolutionary biologist Richard Dawkins offered a potential explanation for the problem of altruism, as first outlined by Darwin in *The Descent of Man*. Darwin had wrestled with the mystery of how selfless kindness toward others might be a positive trait in terms of natural selection and had failed to find an answer in his lifetime.

Dawkins, however, in his landmark book, *The Selfish Gene* (1976), suggested that the unit of selection was not a mammal, reptile, or similar living creature, but its genes. In other words, human beings are merely the carriers for a more enduring life form, the genes themselves, which are practically immortal. Thus, a selfless sacrifice by, say, a childless uncle might preserve, say, a greater proportion of matching genes within his nephews and nieces. In fact, it would not be selfless at all, as the genes would survive.

The "genotype" of directly inherited genes could therefore be superseded by the "phenotype" of broader effects of an individual's environment. Dawkins's theory helps to explain the role not only of altruism in natural selection, but also other human endeavors that might at first seem to be without evolutionary merit, such as charity, the creation of art and literature, and even the existence of religion.

The "Meme"

In the course of his work in *The Selfish Gene*, Dawkins also posited that information itself could exist in discrete units, "breed" through repetition, publication, and rumor, and even "evolve" through mutations such as copying errors and editorial alterations. Dawkins called these pieces of information "memes"; the term itself has flourished and evolved in the 21st century, and is now an integral part of modern slang and Internet custom.

The Weismann Barrier Challenged

Modern biology has also seen a resurgence in Lamarckism. The discovery of the "reverse transcriptase" enzyme has suggested that some retroviruses have the power to physically alter the characteristics of genes. This suggests not only that immune systems can evolve at an exponentially faster rate than previously thought, but also that the "Weismann Barrier" is not absolute. Contrary to the belief of Haeckel (and indeed of Darwin), it could be that some acquired characteristics, such as immunity to particular diseases, can indeed be passed on to descendants via altered genes. This does not threaten Darwin's theory of evolution, but rather suggests that Lamarck's earlier theory of the inheritability of some acquired characteristics may also deserve some credence.

THE ARMY OF BACHELORS
Some have warned that the mapping of the human genome could mark the return of eugenics in a different guise, as it has the potential to enable parents to choose characteristics of their unborn child. Studies have already demonstrated that some parents in certain cultures strongly favor male offspring, to the extent of aborting female fetuses. One fear is that if it becomes possible to preselect a child's sex, this could result in an "army of bachelors," a generation of unmarried men with little hope of finding a partner, with ensuing effects on crime, social welfare, and future generations.

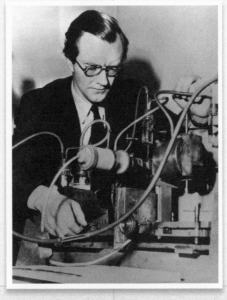

Dr. Maurice Wilkins, who, along with James Watson and Francis Crick, was awarded the 1962 Nobel Prize for Medicine and Physiology "for their discoveries concerning the molecular structure of nucleic acids and its significance for information transfer in living material."

Names and Places

DARWIN IS FOUND ALL OVER THE MODERN WORLD, NOT ONLY IN HIS BOOKS AND THEORIES, BUT IN PLACE-NAMES, ON BANKNOTES AND COINS, AND IN POPULAR CULTURE. TWO HUNDRED YEARS AFTER HIS BIRTH, AND 150 YEARS AFTER THE PUBLICATION OF *ON THE ORIGIN OF SPECIES*, HIS IDEAS STILL IGNITE CONTROVERSY AND INSPIRE RESEARCH. HIS NAME IS A POWERFUL TOKEN IN THE WORLD OF BIOLOGY, AND HAS BEEN LENT TO VENTURES TO THE STARS.

O n January 29, 1833, a glacier on Tierra del Fuego fell into the water opposite a shore party from the *Beagle*. Worried that the resulting wave of water would swamp the boats, Darwin and several men from the ship dragged them out of the shallows to safety. In memory of this brave act, FitzRoy named the inlet Darwin Sound, although Darwin himself confessed that it had not been bravery that motivated him, but fear of being marooned, boatless on Tierra del Fuego. Many other places around the world have likewise been named after Darwin, not only during his voyage, but in the *Beagle*'s subsequent voyage without him, and in years after his death.

On February 12, 1834, aboard the *Beagle*, Captain FitzRoy named the highest peak on Tierra del Fuego Mount Darwin, in honor of Darwin's 25th birthday. There is another Darwin on the Falkland Islands, the site of a battle during the Falklands War. Darwin College in Cambridge was built on land once owned by the Darwin family, whose portraits still hang in it. Among many other places named for the famous scientist, the one with the largest number of inhabitants is the city of Darwin, in north Australia. The area was named by FitzRoy's successor as captain of the *Beagle*, Darwin's former shipmate John Clements Wickham, who arrived in the region in 1839 and named the obscure coastal settlement in Darwin's honor.

As well as place names, Darwin has been honored on currency and postage stamps around the world. He supplanted Charles Dickens on the British ten-pound note in 2003, supposedly because the intricacies of his famous beard made the note harder to forge. In his anniversary year of 2009, he also appeared on a commemorative two-pound coin. Meanwhile, the Falklands' 50-pence piece carries the image of the warrah, the animal whose extinction Darwin predicted.

Units of Evolution
In 1949, the scientist J.B.S. Haldane suggested that evolutionary change could be measured in units, which he called Darwins. The value of a Darwin is calculated by an equation that measures the rate of change in a particular trait over periods of one million years.

Geospiza fortis, the Galápagos bird whose natural selection was observed in real time by scientists in 1977.

"How great would be the desire in every admirer of nature to behold, if such were possible, another planet."

However, not all evolutionary changes take millions of years to occur. On the Galápagos Islands, Darwin's interest in the local birdlife has encouraged other researchers to pay closer attention to the local finches.

During a drought in 1977, the beak of the medium-sized ground finch *Geospiza fortis* was found to grow in size by a factor of 4 per cent. The increased size of beak allowed the finches to eat larger seeds, ensuring that by the end of the drought, finches with the newly evolved beak size greatly outnumbered those with the former, smaller beak.

Other Worlds

Darwin's influence even extends beyond the Earth. The *Beagle 2*, named in honor of the ship that carried him around the world, was an ill-fated probe that lost contact before reaching the surface of Mars in 2006. Darwin has also lent his name to an asteroid, and to a proposed project by the European Space Agency. The Darwin Mission aims to put three space telescopes into formation in orbit, in order to search for evidence of life on planets beyond the solar system. The discovery of life beyond the Earth, and the opportunity to examine the direction of evolution under entirely alien conditions, was something about which Darwin could only have dreamt.

THE DARWIN AWARDS

The Zoological Society of London presents an annual Darwin Award to a student who demonstrates outstanding ability in the field of zoology. However, the prestige of this genuine honor has been overshadowed by a less serious meme: the alternative Darwin Awards. A humorous honor designed to reward those who contribute to the gene pool by removing themselves from it, the Darwin Awards recognize outstanding, often apocryphal, and usually fatal moments of stupidity, including juggling with hand grenades, tying 45 helium balloons to one's chair, and unwisely testing the efficacy of a "stab-proof vest" while wearing it.

"*Ignorance more frequently begets confidence than does knowledge: it is those who know little, and not those who know much, who so positively assert that this or that problem will never be solved by science.*"

— THE DESCENT OF MAN

THE DARWIN CLUB BY REA IRVIN, ONE OF A SERIES ENTITLED,

"Clubs We Do Not Care To Join,"

PUBLISHED IN LIFE, MARCH 18, 1915.

Bibliography and References

Researchers in the 21st century are lucky to have access to a superb Internet-based resource: The Complete Works of Charles Darwin Online, collating not only searchable versions of Darwin's publications in all their variant forms, but much of the correspondence, books that inspired him, illustrations, and explicatory essays. http://darwin-online.org.uk

An enterprise of similar immensity can be found at The Darwin Correspondence Project, which aims to provide an online compendium of every letter written both by and to Darwin. www.darwinproject.ac.uk

Auerbach, J. and Hoffenberg, P. (eds.) *Britain, the Empire, and the World at the Great Exhibition of 1851*. Aldershot: Ashgate, 2008.

Beer, G. *Darwin's Plots: Evolutionary Narrative in Darwin, George Eliot and Nineteeth-Century Fiction*. Cambridge: Cambridge University Press, 2000.

Bowler, P. *The Eclipse of Darwin: Anti-Darwinian Evolution Theories in the Decades around 1900*. Baltimore: Johns Hopkins University Press, 1983.

Browne, J. *Charles Darwin: Voyaging*. London: Pimlico, 2003.

____. *Charles Darwin: The Power of Place*. London: Pimlico, 2003.

Burkhardt, F. (ed.) *Charles Darwin: The Beagle Letters*. Cambridge: Cambridge University Press, 2008.

Cadbury, D. *The Dinosaur Hunters: A True Story of Scientific Rivalry and the Discovery of the Prehistoric World*. London: Fourth Estate, 2001.

Cobbe, F. *Life of Frances Power Cobbe, as Told by Herself, with Additions by the Author*. London: Swan Sonnenschein, 1904.

Colp, R. *Darwin's Illness*. Gainesville: University Press of Florida, 2008.

Darwin, C. *Autobiographies*. Harmondsworth: Penguin, 2002.

Dawkins, R. *The Selfish Gene*, 2nd edition. Oxford: Oxford University Press, 1989.

____. *The Extended Phenotype*. Oxford: Oxford University Press, 1989.

____. *The Blind Watchmaker: Why the Evidence of Evolution Reveals a Universe Without Design*. Harmondsworth: Penguin, 1999.

____. *River Out of Eden: A Darwinian View of Life*. London: Phoenix, 2001.

Desmond, A. and Moore, J. *Darwin*. Harmondsworth: Penguin, 1991.

____. *Darwin's Sacred Curse: Race, Slavery and the Quest for Human Origins*. Harmondsworth: Allen Lane, 2009.

Johnson, P. *Darwin on Trial*. Westmont, Illinois: InterVarsity Press, 1993.

Keynes, R. *Annie's Box: Charles Darwin, His Daughter and Human Evolution*. London: Fourth Estate, 2001.

Lustig, A. "George Eliot, Charles Darwin and the Labyrinth of History," in *Endeavour*, Vol. 23, no. 3, 1999, pp. 110–13.

Raby, P. *Alfred Russel Wallace: A Life*. Princeton: Princeton University Press, 2002.

Slotten, R. *The Heretic in Darwin's Court: The Life of Alfred Russel Wallace*. New York: Columbia University Press, 2006.

Steele, E. et al. *Lamarck's Signature: How Retrogenes are Changing Darwin's Natural Selection Paradigm*. Sydney: Allen & Unwin, 1998.

Stott, R. *Darwin and the Barnacle*. London: Faber and Faber, 2003.

Wilson, E. (ed.) *From So Simple a Beginning: The Four Great Books of Charles Darwin*. New York: Norton, 2006.

Index

Credits

All original artwork by Rob Brandt © Quid Publishing. (PD = public domain images) Other images credited as follows:

Page 3 left reproduced with permission from John van Wyhe ed., The Complete Work of Charles Darwin Online (http://darwin-online.org.uk/)
Page 3 right © Bettmann/CORBIS
Page 5 Library of Congress Prints and Photographs Division
Page 7 Library of Congress Prints and Photographs Division
Page 9 Library of Congress Prints and Photographs Division
Page 10 PD
Page 12 PD
Page 15 PD
Page 16 © Kaidokarner | Dreamstime.com
Page 21 from Library of Congress Prints and Photographs Division
Page 22 reproduced with acknowledgement to Peter Stubbs. (www.edinphoto.org.uk)
Page 25 PD
Page 26 PD
Page 27 PD
Page 31 top PD
Page 31 bottom PD
Page 32 PD
Page 34 reproduced with permission from John van Wyhe ed., The Complete Work of Charles Darwin Online (http://darwin-online.org.uk/)
Page 37 Library of Congress Prints and Photographs Division
Page 38 PD
Page 39 portraits reproduced with permission from John van Wyhe ed., The Complete Work of Charles Darwin Online (http://darwin-online.org.uk/)
Page 43 PD
Page 45 PD
Page 47 reproduced with permission from John van Wyhe ed., The Complete Work of Charles Darwin Online (http://darwin-online.org.uk/)
Page 51 bottom © Mortenelm | Dreamstime.com
Page 54 PD
Page 55 left Library and Archives Canada
Page 55 right Library and Archives Canada
Page 57 © Stapleton Collection/Corbis
Page 59 Library of Congress Prints and Photographs Division
Page 60 PD
Page 61 top © Bettmann/CORBIS
Page 61 right PD
Page 62 right PD
Page 65 bottom reproduced with permission from John van Wyhe ed., The Complete Work of Charles Darwin Online (http://darwin-online.org.uk/)
Page 66 PD
Page 67 top PD
Page 67 bottom PD
Page 69 PD
Page 70 left PD
Page 70 right PD
Page 71 reproduced by kind permission of the Syndics of Cambridge University Library
Page 73 left reproduced with permission from John van Wyhe ed., The Complete Work of Charles Darwin Online (http://darwin-online.org.uk/)
Page 75 © David Ball/CORBIS
Page 76 top PD
Page 76 bottom PD
Page 77 left PD
Page 77 right PD
Page 79 left reproduced with permission from John van Wyhe ed., The Complete Work of Charles Darwin Online (http://darwin-online.org.uk/)
Page 79 right reproduced with permission from John van Wyhe ed., The Complete Work of Charles Darwin Online (http://darwin-online.org.uk/)
Page 81 reproduced with permission from John van Wyhe ed., The Complete Work of Charles Darwin Online (http://darwin-online.org.uk/)
Page 83 top reproduced by kind permission of the Syndics of Cambridge University Library
Page 84 PD
Page 85 top PD
Page 87 Library of Congress Prints and Photographs Division
Page 89 top © CORBIS
Page 90 PD
Page 91 top PD
Page 91 bottom PD
Page 93 bottom PD
Page 95 top PD
Page 95 bottom PD
Page 96 left © Historical Picture Archive/CORBIS
Page 96 right PD
Page 99 right PD
Page 101 PD
Page 103 Library of Congress Prints and Photographs Division
Page 104 top PD
Page 104 bottom PD
Page 105 top PD
Page 105 centre PD
Page 105 bottom PD
Page 106 PD
Page 107 © Michael Nicholson/CORBIS
Page 108 PD
Page 109 © 2007 Getty Images
Page 111 top PD
Page 111 bottom PD
Page 112 PD
Page 113 © Sibrikov | Dreamstime.com
Page 114 PD
Page 115 top © Bettmann/CORBIS
Page 116 PD
Page 117 PD
Page 119 Library of Congress Prints and Photographs Division
Page 120 reproduced with permission from John van Wyhe ed., The Complete Work of Charles Darwin Online (http://darwin-online.org.uk/)
Page 123 © Bright | Dreamstime.com
Page 124 PD
Page 125 PD
Page 126 reproduced with permission from John van Wyhe ed., The Complete Work of Charles Darwin Online (http://darwin-online.org.uk/)
Page 127 reproduced with permission from John van Wyhe ed., The Complete Work of Charles Darwin Online (http://darwin-online.org.uk/)
Page 129 reproduced with permission from John van Wyhe ed., The Complete Work of Charles Darwin Online (http://darwin-online.org.uk/)
Page 131 PD
Page 133 PD
Page 134 PD
Page 135 bottom PD
Page 137 PD
Page 139 Library of Congress Prints and Photographs Division
Page 140 bottom PD
Page 141 top PD
Page 142 PD
Page 143 top Library and Archives Canada
Page 145 top left © Bettmann/CORBIS
Page 145 bottom © Jonathan Clements
Page 147 top PD
Page 147 bottom PD
Page 148 PD
Page 149 © 2008 Getty Images
Page 150 PD
Page 151 © Atman | Dreamstime.com
Page 153 © Bettmann/CORBIS
Page 155 PD
Page 156 Library of Congress Prints and Photographs Division